Tertullian
On the Resurrection of the Flesh

Tertullian
On the Resurrection of the Flesh

Tertullian
On the Resurrection of the Flesh

© Lighthouse Publishing 2018

Written by: Tertullian (155 – 240)

Translated by: Dr. Peter Holmes (1815 – 1878)

Updated into Modern U.S English by A.M. Overett B.A., REL (b. 1960)

Published by
Lighthouse Christian Publishing
SAN 257-4330
5531 Dufferin Drive
Savage, Minnesota, 55378
United States of America

www.lighthousechristianpublishing.com

On the Resurrection of the Flesh.

The heretics against whom this work is directed, were the same who maintained that the demiurge, or the god who created this world and gave the Mosaic dispensation, was opposed to the supreme God. Hence they attached an idea of inherent corruption and worthlessness to all his works—amongst the rest, to the flesh or body of man; affirming that it could not rise again, and that the soul alone was capable of inheriting immortality.

Chapter I.—The Doctrine of the Resurrection of the Body Brought to Light by the Gospel. The Faintest Glimpses of Something Like It Occasionally Met with in Heathenism. Inconsistencies of Pagan Teaching.

The resurrection of the dead is the Christian's trust. By it we are believers. To the belief of this (article of the faith) truth compels us—that truth which God reveals, but the crowd derides, which supposes that nothing will survive after death. And yet they do honor to their dead, and that too in the most expensive way according to their bequest, and with the daintiest banquets which the seasons can produce, on the presumption that those whom they declare to be incapable of all perception still retain an appetite. But (let the crowd deride): I on my side must deride it still more, especially when it burns up its dead with harshest inhumanity, only to pamper them immediately afterwards with gluttonous satiety, using the selfsame fires to honor them and to insult them. What piety is that which mocks its victims with cruelty? Is it sacrifice or insult (which the crowd offers), when it burns its offerings to those it has already burnt? But the wise, too, join with the vulgar crowd in their opinion sometimes. There is nothing after death, according to the school of Epicurus. After death all things come to an end, even death itself, says Seneca to like effect. It is satisfactory, however, that the no less important philosophy of Pythagoras and Empedocles, and the Plantonists, take the contrary view, and declare the soul to be immortal; affirming, moreover, in a way which most nearly approaches (to our own doctrine), that the soul actually returns into bodies, although not the same bodies, and not even those of human beings invariably: thus Euphorbus is supposed to have passed into Phythagoras, and Homer into a peacock. They firmly pronounced the soul's renewal to be in a body, (deeming it) more tolerable to change the quality (of the corporeal state) than to deny it wholly: they at least knocked at the door of truth, although they entered not. Thus the world, with all its errors, does not ignore the resurrection of the dead.

Chapter II. —The Jewish Sadducees a Link Between the Pagan Philosophers and the Heretics on This Doctrine. Its Fundamental Importance Asserted. The Soul Fares Better Than the Body, in Heretical Estimation, as to Its Future State. Its Extinction, However, Was Held by One Lucan.

Since there is even within the confines of God's Church a sect which is more nearly allied to the Epicureans than to the prophets, an opportunity is afforded us of knowing what estimate Christ forms of the (said sect, even the) Sadducees. For to Christ was it reserved to lay bare everything which before was concealed: to impart certainty to doubtful points; to accomplish those of which men had had but a foretaste; to give present reality to the objects of prophecy; and to furnish not only by Himself, but actually in Himself, certain proofs of the resurrection of the dead. It is, however, against other Sadducees that we have now to prepare ourselves, but still partakers of their doctrine. For instance, they allow a moiety of the resurrection; that is, simply of the soul, despising the flesh, just as they also do the Lord of the flesh Himself. No other persons, indeed, refuse to concede to the substance of the body its recovery from death, heretical inventors of a second deity. Driven then, as they are, to give a different dispensation to Christ, so that He may not be accounted as belonging to the Creator, they have achieved their first error in the article of His very flesh; contending with Marcion and Basilides that it possessed no reality; or else holding, after the heretical tenets of Valentinus, and according to Apelles, that it had qualities peculiar to itself. And so it follows that they shut out from all recovery from death that substance of which they say that Christ did not partake, confidently assuming that it furnishes the strongest presumption against the resurrection, since the flesh is already risen in Christ. Hence it is that we have ourselves previously issued our volume On the flesh of Christ; in which we both furnish proofs of its reality, in opposition to the idea of its being a vain phantom; and claim for it a human nature without any peculiarity of condition—such a nature as has marked out Christ to be both man and the Son of man. For when we prove Him to be invested with the flesh and in a bodily condition, we at the same time refute heresy, by establishing the rule that no other being than the Creator must be believed to be God, since we show that Christ, in whom God is plainly discerned, is precisely of such a nature as the Creator promised that He should be. Being thus refuted touching God as the Creator, and Christ as the Redeemer of the flesh, they will at once be defeated also on the resurrection of the flesh. No procedure, indeed, can be more reasonable. And we affirm that controversy with heretics should in most cases be conducted in this way. For due method requires that conclusions should always be drawn from the most important premises, in order that there be a prior agreement on the essential point, by means of which the particular question under review may be said to have been determined. Hence it is that the heretics, from their conscious weakness, never conduct discussion in an orderly manner. They are well aware how hard is their task in insinuating the existence of a second god, to the disparagement of the Creator of the world, who is known to all men naturally by the testimony of His works, who is before all others in the mysteries of His being, and is especially manifested in the prophets; then, under the pretense of considering a more urgent inquiry, namely man's own salvation—a question which transcends all others in its importance—they begin with doubts about the resurrection; for there is greater difficulty in believing the resurrection of the flesh than the oneness of the Deity. In this way, after they have deprived the discussion of the advantages of its logical order, and have embarrassed it with doubtful insinuations in disparagement of the flesh, they gradually draw their argument to the reception of a second god after destroying and changing the very ground of our hopes. For when once a man is fallen or removed from the sure hope which he had placed in the Creator, he is easily led away to the object of a different hope, whom however of his own accord he can hardly help suspecting. Now it is by a discrepancy in the promises that a difference of gods is insinuated. How many do we thus see drawn into the net vanquished on the resurrection of the flesh, before they could carry their point on the oneness of the Deity! In respect, then, of the heretics, we have shown with what weapons we ought to meet them. And indeed we have already encountered them in treatises severally directed against them: on the one only God and His Christ, in our work against Marcion, on the Lord's flesh, in our book against the four heresies, for the special purpose of opening the way to the present inquiry: so that we have now only to discuss the resurrection of the flesh, (treating it) just as if it were uncertain in regard to ourselves also, that is, in the system of the Creator. Because many persons are uneducated; still more are of faltering faith, and several are weak-minded: these will have to be instructed, directed, strengthened, inasmuch as the very oneness of the Godhead will be defended along with the maintenance of our doctrine. For if the resurrection of the flesh be denied, that prime article of the faith is shaken; if it be asserted, that is established. There is no need, I suppose, to treat of the soul's safety; for nearly all the heretics, in whatever way they conceive of it, certainly refrain from denying that. We may ignore a certain Lucan, who does not spare even this part of our nature, which he follows Aristotle in reducing to dissolution, and substitutes some other thing in lieu of it. Some third nature it is which, according to him, is to rise again, neither soul nor flesh; in other words, not man, but a bear perhaps—for instance, Lucan himself. Even he has received from us a copious notice in our book on the entire condition of the soul, the especial immortality of which we there maintain, whilst we also both acknowledge the dissolution of the flesh alone, and emphatically assert its restitution. Into the body of that work were collected whatever points we elsewhere had to reserve from the pressure of incidental causes. For as it is my custom to touch some questions but lightly on their first occurrence, so I am obliged also to postpone the consideration of them, until the outline can be filled in with complete detail, and the deferred points be taken up on their own merits.

Chapter III. —Some Truths Held Even by the Heathen. They Were, However, More Often Wrong Both in Religious Opinions and in Moral Practice. The Heathen Not to Be Followed in Their Ignorance of the Christian Mystery. The Heretics Perversely Prone to Follow Them.

One may no doubt be wise in the things of God, even from one's natural powers, but only in witness to the truth, not in maintenance of error; (only) when one acts in accordance with, not in opposition to, the divine dispensation. For some things are known even by nature: the immortality of the soul, for instance, is held by many; the knowledge of our God is possessed by all. I may use, therefore, the opinion of a Plato, when he declares, "Every soul is immortal." I may use also the conscience of a nation, when it attests the God of gods. I may, in like manner, use all the other intelligences of our common nature, when they pronounce God to be a judge. "God sees," (say they); and, "I commend you to God." But when they say, "What has undergone death is dead," and, "Enjoy life whilst you live," and, "After death all things come to an end, even death itself;" then I must remember both that "the heart of man is ashes," according to the estimate of God, and that the very "Wisdom of the world is foolishness," (as the inspired word) pronounces it to be. Then, if even the heretic seek refuge in the depraved thoughts of the vulgar, or the imaginations of the world, I must say to him: Part company with the heathen, O heretic! for although you are all agreed in imagining a God, yet while you do so in the name of Christ, so long as you deem yourself a Christian, you are a different man from a heathen: give him back his own views of things, since he does not himself learn from yours. Why lean upon a blind guide, if you have eyes of your own? Why be clothed by one who is naked, if you have put on Christ? Why use the shield of another, when the apostle gives you armor of your own? It would be better for him to learn from you to acknowledge the resurrection of the flesh, than for you from him to deny it; because if Christians must needs deny it, it would be sufficient if they did so from their own knowledge, without any instruction from the ignorant multitude. He, therefore, will not be a Christian who shall deny this doctrine which is confessed by Christians; denying it, moreover, on grounds which are adopted by a man who is not a Christian. Take away, indeed, from the heretics the wisdom which they share with the heathen, and let them support their inquiries from the Scriptures alone: they will then be unable to keep their ground. For that which commends men's common sense is its very simplicity, and its participation in the same feelings, and its community of opinions; and it is deemed to be all the more trustworthy, inasmuch as its definitive statements are naked and open, and known to all. Divine reason, on the contrary, lies in the very pith and marrow of things, not on the surface, and very often is at variance with appearances.

Chapter IV. —Heathens and Heretics Alike in Their Vilification of the Flesh and Its Functions, the Ordinary Cavils Against the Final Restitution of So Weak and Ignoble a Substance.

Hence it is that heretics start at once from this point, from which they sketch the first draft of their dogmas, and afterwards add the details, being well aware how easily men's minds are caught by its influence, (and actuated) by that community of human sentiment which is so favorable to their designs. Is there anything else that you can hear of from the heretic, as also from the heathen, earlier in time or greater in extent? Is not (their burden) from the beginning and everywhere an invective against the flesh—against its origin, against its substance, against the casualties and the invariable end which await it; unclean from its first formation of the dregs of the ground, uncleaner afterwards from the mire of its own seminal transmission; worthless, weak, covered with guilt, laden with misery, full of trouble; and after all this record of its degradation, dropping into its original earth and the appellation of a corpse, and destined to dwindle away even from this loathsome name into none henceforth at all—into the very death of all designation? Now you are a shrewd man, no doubt: will you then persuade yourself, that after this flesh has been withdrawn from sight, and touch, and memory, it can never be rehabilitated from corruption to integrity, from a shattered to a solid state, from an empty to a full condition, from nothing at all to something—the devouring fires, and the waters of the sea, and the maws of beasts, and the crops of birds and the stomachs of fishes, and time's own great paunch itself of course yielding it all up again? Shall the same flesh which has fallen to decay be so expected to recover, as that the lame, and the one-eyed, and the blind, and the leper, and the palsied shall come back again, although there can be no pleasure in returning to their old condition? Or shall they be whole, and so have to fear exposure to such sufferings? What, in that case, (must we say) of the consequences of resuming the flesh? Will it again be subject to all its present wants, especially meats and drinks? Shall we have with our lungs to float (in air or water), and suffer pain in our bowels, and with organs of shame to feel no shame, and with all our limbs to toil and labor? Must there again be ulcers, and wounds, and fever, and gout, and once more the wishing to die? Of course these will be the longings incident on the recovery of the flesh, only the repetition of desires to escape out of it. Well now, we have (stated) all this in very subdued and delicate phrases, as suited to the character of our style; but (would you know) how great a license of unseemly language these men actually use, you must test them in their conferences, whether they be heathens or heretics.

Chapter V.—Some Considerations in Reply Eulogistic of the Flesh. It Was Created by God. The Body of Man Was, in Fact, Previous to His Soul.

Inasmuch as all uneducated men, therefore, still form their opinions after these commonsense views, and as the falterers and the weak-minded have a renewal of their perplexities occasioned by the selfsame views; and as the first battering-ram which is directed against ourselves is that which shatters the condition of the flesh, we must on our side necessarily so manage our defenses, as to guard, first of all, the condition of the flesh, their disparagement of it being repulsed by our own eulogy. The heretics, therefore, challenged us to use our rhetoric no less than our philosophy. Respecting, then, this frail and poor, worthless body, which they do not indeed hesitate to call evil, even if it had been the work of angels, as Menander and Marcus are pleased to think, or the formation of some fiery being, an angel, as Apelles teaches, it would be quite enough for securing respect for the body, that it had the support and protection of even a secondary deity. The angels, we know, rank next to God. Now, whatever be the supreme

God of each heretic, I should not unfairly derive the dignity of the flesh likewise from Him to whom was present the will for its production. For, of course, if He had not willed its production, He would have prohibited it, when He knew it was in progress. It follows, then, that even on their principle the flesh is equally the work of God. There is no work but belongs to Him who has permitted it to exist. It is indeed a happy circumstance, that most of their doctrines, including even the harshest, accord to our God the entire formation of man. How mighty He is, you know full well who believe that He is the only God. Let, then, the flesh begin to give you pleasure, since the Creator thereof is so great. But, you say, even the world is the work of God, and yet "the fashion of this world passeth away," as the apostle himself testifies; nor must it be predetermined that the world will be restored, simply because it is the work of God. And surely if the universe, after its ruin, is not to be formed again, why should a portion of it be? You are right, if a portion is on an equality with the whole. But we maintain that there is a difference. In the first place, because all things were made by the Word of God, and without Him was nothing made. Now the flesh, too, had its existence from the Word of God, because of the principle, that here should be nothing without that Word. "Let us make man," said He, before He created him, and added, "with our hand," for the sake of his pre-eminence, that so he might not be compared with the rest of creation. And "God," says (the Scripture), "formed man." There is undoubtedly a great difference in the procedure, springing of course from the nature of the case. For the creatures which were made were inferior to him for whom they were made; and they were made for man, to whom they were afterwards made subject by God. Rightly, therefore, had the creatures which were thus intended for subjection, come forth into being at the bidding and command and sole power of the divine voice; whilst man, on the contrary, destined to be their lord, was formed by God Himself, to the intent that he might be able to exercise his mastery, being created by the

Master the Lord Himself. Remember, too, that man is properly called flesh, which had a prior occupation in man's designation: "And God formed man the clay of the ground." He now became man, who was hitherto clay. "And He breathed upon his face the breath of life, and man (that is, the clay) became a living soul; and God placed the man whom He had formed in the garden." So that man was clay at first, and only afterwards man entire. I wish to impress this on your attention, with a view to your knowing, that whatever God has at all purposed or promised to man, is due not to the soul simply, but to the flesh also; if not arising out of any community in their origin, yet at all events by the privilege possessed by the latter in its name.

Chapter VI. —Not the Lowliness of the Material, But the Dignity and Skill of the Maker, Must Be Remembered, in Gauging the Excellence of the Flesh. Christ Partook of Our Flesh.

Let me therefore pursue the subject before me—if I can but succeed in vindicating for the flesh as much as was conferred on it by Him who made it, glorying as it even then was, because that poor paltry material, clay, found its way into the hands of God, whatever these were, happy enough at merely being touched by them. But why this glorying? Was it that, without any further labor, the clay had instantly assumed its form at the touch of God? The truth is, a great matter was in progress, out of which the creature under consideration was being fashioned. So often then does it receive honor, as often as it experiences the hands of God, when it is touched by them, and pulled, and drawn out, and molded into shape. Imagine God wholly employed and absorbed in it—in His hand, His eye, His labor, His purpose, His wisdom, His providence, and above all, in His love, which was dictating the lineaments (of this creature). For, whatever was the form and expression which was then given to the clay (by the Creator) Christ was in

His thoughts as one day to become man, because the Word, too, was to be both clay and flesh, even as the earth was then. For so did the Father previously say to the Son: "Let us make man in our own image, after our likeness." And God made man, that is to say, the creature which He molded and fashioned; after the image of God (in other words, of Christ) did He make him. And the Word was God also, who being in the image of God, "thought it not robbery to be equal to God." Thus, that clay which was even then putting on the image of Christ, who was to come in the flesh, was not only the work, but also the pledge and surety, of God. To what purpose is it to bandy about the name earth, as that of a sordid and groveling element, with the view of tarnishing the origin of the flesh, when, even if any other material had been available for forming man, it would be requisite that the dignity of the Maker should be taken into consideration, who even by His selection of His material deemed it, and by His management made it, worthy? The hand of Phidias forms the Olympian Jupiter of ivory; worship is given to the statue, and it is no longer regarded as a god formed out of a silliest animal, but as the world's supreme Deity—not because of the bulk of the elephant, but on account of the renown of Phidias. Could not therefore the living God, the true God, purge away by His own operation whatever vileness might have accrued to His material, and heal it of all infirmity? Or must this remain to show how much more nobly man could fabricate a god, than God could form a man? Now, although the clay is offensive (for its poorness), it is now something else. What I possess is flesh, not earth, even although of the flesh it is said: "Dust thou art, and unto dust shalt thou return." In these words, there is the mention of the origin, not a recalling of the substance. The privilege has been granted to the flesh to be nobler than its origin, and to have happiness aggrandized by the change wrought in it. Now, even gold is earth, because of the earth; but it remains earth no longer after it becomes gold, but is a far different substance, more splendid and more noble, though coming from a source which is comparatively faded and obscure. In like manner, it was quite allowable for God that He should clear the gold of our flesh from all the taints, as you deem them, of its native clay, by purging the original substance of its dross.

Chapter VII. —The Earthy Material of Which Flesh is Created Wonderfully Improved by God's Manipulation. By the Addition of the Soul in Man's Constitution It Became the Chief Work in the Creation.

But perhaps the dignity of the flesh may seem to be diminished, because it has not been actually manipulated by the hand of God, as the clay was at first. Now, when God handled the clay for the express purpose of the growth of flesh out of it afterwards, it was for the flesh that He took all the trouble. But I want you, moreover, to know at what time and in what manner the flesh flourished into beauty out of its clay. For it cannot be, as some will have it, that those "coats of skins" which Adam and Eve put on when they were stripped of paradise, were really themselves the forming of the flesh out of clay, because long before that Adam had already recognized the flesh which was in the woman as the propagation of his own substance ("This is now bone of my bone, and flesh of my flesh"), and the very taking of the woman out of the man was supplemented with flesh; but it ought, I should suppose, to have been made good with clay, if Adam was still clay. The clay, therefore, was obliterated and absorbed into flesh. When did this happen? At the time that man became a living soul by the inbreathing of God—by the breath indeed which was capable of hardening clay into another substance, as into some earthenware, so now into flesh. In the same way the potter, too, has it in his power, by tempering the blast of his fire, to modify his clayey material into a stiffer one, and to mold one form after another more beautiful than the original substance, and now possessing both a kind and name of its own. For although the Scripture says, "Shall the clay say to the potter?" that is,

Shall man contend with God? although the apostle speaks of "earthen vessels" he refers to man, who was originally clay. And the vessel is the flesh, because this was made of clay by the breath of the divine afflatus; and it was afterwards clothed with "the coats of skins," that is, with the cutaneous covering which was placed over it. So truly is this the fact, that if you withdraw the skin, you lay bare the flesh. Thus, that which becomes a spoil when stripped off, was a vestment as long as it remained laid over. Hence the apostle, when he calls circumcision "a putting off (or spoliation) of the flesh," affirmed the skin to be a coat or tunic. Now this being the case, you have both the clay made glorious by the hand of God, and the flesh more glorious still by His breathing upon it, by virtue of which the flesh not only laid aside its clayey rudiments, but also took on itself the ornaments of the soul. You surely are not more careful than God, that you indeed should refuse to mount the gems of Scythia and India and the pearls of the Red Sea in lead, or brass, or iron, or even in silver, but should set them in the most precious and most highly-wrought gold; or, again, that you should provide for your finest wines and most costly unguents the most fitting vessels; or, on the same principle, should find for your swords of finished temper scabbards of equal worth; whilst God must consign to some vilest sheath the shadow of His own soul, the breath of His own Spirit, the operation of His own mouth, and by so ignominious a consignment secure, of course, its condemnation. Well, then, has He placed, or rather inserted and commingled, it with the flesh? Yes; and so intimate is the union, that it may be deemed to be uncertain whether the flesh bears about the soul, or the soul the flesh; or whether the flesh acts as apparitor to the soul, or the soul to the flesh. It is, however, more credible that the soul has service rendered to it, and has the mastery, as being more proximate in character to God. This circumstance even redounds to the glory of the flesh, inasmuch as it both contains an essence nearest to God's, and renders itself a partaker of (the soul's) actual sovereignty. For what enjoyment of nature is there, what produce of the world, what relish of the elements, which is not imparted to the soul by means of the body? How can it be otherwise? Is it not by its means that the soul is supported by the entire apparatus of the senses—the sight, the hearing, the taste, the smell, the touch? Is it not by its means that it has a sprinkling of the divine power, there being nothing which it does not effect by its faculty of speech, even when it is only tacitly indicated? And speech is the result of a fleshly organ. The arts come through the flesh; through the flesh also effect is given to the mind's pursuits and powers; all work, too, and business and offices of life, are accomplished by the flesh; and so utterly are the living acts of the soul the work of the flesh, that for the soul to cease to do living acts, would be nothing else than sundering itself from the flesh. So also the very act of dying is a function of the flesh, even as the process of life is. Now, if all things are subject to the soul through the flesh, their subjection is equally due to the flesh. That which is the means and agent of your enjoyment, must needs be also the partaker and sharer of your enjoyment. So that the flesh, which is accounted the minister and servant of the soul, turns out to be also its associate and co-heir. And if all this in temporal things, why not also in things eternal?

Chapter VIII. —Christianity, by Its Provision for the Flesh, Has Put on It the Greatest Honor. The Privileges of Our Religion in Closest Connection with Our Flesh. Which Also Bears a Large Share in the Duties and Sacrifices of Religion.

Now such remarks have I wished to advance in defense of the flesh, from a general view of the condition of our human nature. Let us now consider its special relation to Christianity, and see how vast a privilege before God has been conferred on this poor and worthless substance. It would suffice to say, indeed, that there is not a soul that can at all procure salvation, except it believes whilst it is in the flesh, so true is it that the flesh is the very condition on which salvation hinges. And since the soul is, in consequence of its salvation, chosen to the service of God, it is the flesh which actually renders it capable of such service. The flesh, indeed, is washed, in order that the soul may be cleansed; the flesh is anointed, that the soul may be consecrated; the flesh is signed (with the cross), that the soul too may be fortified; the flesh is shadowed with the imposition of hands, that the soul also maybe illuminated by the Spirit; the flesh feeds on the body and blood of Christ, that the soul likewise may fatten on its God. They cannot then be separated in their recompense, when they are united in their service. Those sacrifices, moreover, which are acceptable to God—I mean conflicts of the soul, fastings, and abstinences, and the humiliations which are annexed to such duty—it is the flesh which performs again and again to its own especial suffering. Virginity, likewise, and widowhood, and the modest restraint in secret on the marriage-bed, and the one only adoption of it, are fragrant offerings to God paid out of the good services of the flesh. Come, tell me what is your opinion of the flesh, when it has to contend for the name of Christ, dragged out to public view, and exposed to the hatred of all men; when it pines in prisons under the cruelest privation of light, in banishment from the world, amidst squalor, filth, and noisome food, without freedom even in sleep, for it is bound on its very pallet and mangled in its bed of straw; when at length before the public view it is racked by every kind of torture that can be devised, and when finally it is spent beneath its agonies, struggling to render its last turn for Christ by dying for Him— upon His own cross many times, not to say by still more atrocious devices of torment. Most blessed, truly, and most glorious, must be the flesh which can repay its Master Christ so vast a debt, and so completely, that the only obligation remaining due to Him is, that it should cease by death to owe Him more—all the more bound even then in gratitude, because (forever) set free.

Chapter IX. —God's Love for the Flesh of Man, as Developed in the Grace of Christ Towards It. The Flesh the Best Means of Displaying the Bounty and Power of God.

To recapitulate, then: Shall that very flesh, which the Divine Creator formed with His own hands in the image of God; which He animated with His own afflatus, after the likeness of His own vital vigor; which He set over all the works of His hand, to dwell amongst, to enjoy, and to rule them; which He clothed with His sacraments and His instructions; whose purity He loves, whose mortifications He approves; whose sufferings for Himself He deems precious;—(shall that flesh, I say), so often brought near to God, not rise again? God forbid, God forbid, (I repeat), that He should abandon to everlasting destruction the labor of His own hands, the care of His own thoughts, the receptacle of His own Spirit, the queen of His creation, the inheritor of His own liberality, the priestess of His religion, the champion of His testimony, the sister of His Christ! We know by experience the goodness of God; from His Christ we learn that He is the only God, and the very good. Now, as He requires from us love to our neighbor after love to Himself, so He will Himself do that which He has commanded. He will love the flesh which is, so very closely and in so many ways, His neighbor—(He will love it), although infirm, since His strength is made perfect in weakness; although disordered, since "they that are whole need not the physician, but they that are sick;" although not honorable, since "we bestow more abundant honor upon the less honorable members;" although ruined, since He says, "I am come to save that which was lost;" although sinful, since He says, "I desire rather the salvation of the sinner than his death;" although condemned, for says He, "I shall wound, and also heal." Why reproach the flesh with those conditions which wait for God, which hope in God, which receive honor from God, which He succors? I venture to declare, that if such casualties as these had never befallen the flesh, the bounty, the grace, the mercy, (and indeed) all the beneficent power of God, would have had no opportunity to work.

Chapter X.—Holy Scripture Magnifies the Flesh, as to Its Nature and Its Prospects.

You hold to the scriptures in which the flesh is disparaged; receive also those in which it is ennobled. You read whatever passage abases it; direct your eyes also to that which elevates it. "All flesh is grass." Well, but Isaiah was not content to say only this; but he also declared, "All flesh shall see the salvation of God." They notice God when He says in Genesis, "My Spirit shall not remain among these men, because they are flesh;" but then He is also heard saying by Joel, "I will pour out of my Spirit upon all flesh." Even the apostle ought not to be known for any one statement in which he is wont to reproach the flesh. For although he says that "in his flesh dwelleth no good thing;" although he affirms that "they who are in the flesh cannot please God," because "the flesh lusteth against the Spirit;" yet in these and similar assertions which he makes, it is not the substance of the flesh, but its actions, which are censured. Moreover, we shall elsewhere take occasion to remark, that no reproaches can fairly be cast upon the flesh, without tending also to the castigation of the soul, which compels the flesh to do its bidding. However, let me meanwhile add that in the same passage Paul "carries about in his body the marks of the Lord Jesus;" he also forbids our body to be profaned, as being "the temple of God;" he makes our bodies "the members of Christ;" and he exhorts us to exalt and "glorify God in our body." If, therefore, the humiliations of the flesh thrust off its resurrection, why shall not its high prerogatives rather avail to bring it about? —since it better suits the character of God to restore to salvation what for a while He rejected, than to surrender to perdition what He once approved.

Chapter XI. —The Power of God Fully Competent to Effect the Resurrection of the Flesh.

Thus far touching my eulogy of the flesh, in opposition to its enemies, who are, notwithstanding, its greatest friends also; for there is nobody who lives so much in accordance with the flesh as they who deny the resurrection of the flesh, inasmuch as they despise all its discipline, while they disbelieve its punishment. It is a shrewd saying which the Paraclete utters concerning these persons by the mouth of the prophetess Prisca: "They are carnal, and yet they hate the flesh." Since, then, the flesh has the best guarantee that could possibly accrue for securing to it the recompense of salvation, ought we not also to consider well the power, and might, and competency of God Himself, whether He be so great as to be able to rebuild and restore the edifice of the flesh, which had become dilapidated and blocked up, and in every possible way dislocated?—whether He has promulgated in the public domains of nature any analogies to convince us of His power in this respect, lest any should happen to be still thirsting for the knowledge of God, when faith in Him must rest on no other basis than the belief that He is able to do all things? You have, no doubt amongst your philosopher's men who maintain that this world is without a beginning or a maker. It is, however, much more true, that nearly all the heresies allow it an origin and a maker, and ascribe its creation to our God. Firmly believe, therefore, that He produced it wholly out of nothing, and then you have found the knowledge of God, by believing that He possesses such mighty power. But some persons are too weak to believe all this at first, owing to their views about Matter. They will rather have it, after the philosophers, that the universe was in the beginning made by God out of underlying matter. Now, even if this opinion could be held in truth, since He must be acknowledged to have produced in His reformation of matter far different substances and far different forms from those which Matter itself possessed, I should maintain, with no less persistence, that He produced these things out of nothing, since they absolutely had no existence at all previous to His production of them. Now, where is the difference between a thing's being produced out of nothing or out of something, if so be that what existed not comes into being, when even to have had no existence is tantamount to having been nothing? The contrary is likewise true; for having once existed amounts to having been something. If, however, there is a difference, both alternatives support my position. For if God produced all things whatever out of nothing, He will be able to draw forth from nothing even the flesh which had fallen into nothing; or if He molded other things out of matter, He will be able to call forth the flesh too from somewhere else, into whatever abyss it may have been engulfed. And surely He is most competent to re-create who created, inasmuch as it is a far greater work to have produced than to have reproduced, to have imparted a beginning, than to have maintained a continuance. On this principle, you may be quite sure that the restoration of the flesh is easier than its first formation.

Chapter XII. —Some Analogies in Nature Which Corroborate the Resurrection of the Flesh.

Consider now those very analogies of the divine power (to which we have just alluded). Day dies into night, and is buried everywhere in darkness. The glory of the world is obscured in the shadow of death; its entire substance is tarnished with blackness; all things become sordid, silent, stupid; everywhere business ceases, and occupations rest. And so over the loss of the light there is mourning. But yet it again revives, with its own beauty, its own dowry, is own sun, the same as ever, whole and entire, over all the world, slaying its own death, night—opening its own sepulcher, the darkness—coming forth the heir to itself, until the night also revives—it, too, accompanied with a retinue of its own. For the stellar rays are rekindled, which had been quenched in the morning glow; the distant groups of the constellations are again brought back to view, which the day's temporary interval had removed out of sight. Readorned also are the mirrors of the moon, which her monthly course had worn away. Winters and summers return, as do the spring-tide and autumn, with their resources, their routines, their fruits. Forasmuch as earth receives its instruction from heaven to clothe the trees which had been stripped, to color the flowers afresh, to spread the grass again, to reproduce the seed which had been consumed, and not to reproduce them until consumed. Wondrous method! from a defrauder to be a preserver, in order to restore, it takes away; in order to guard, it destroys; that it may make whole, it injures; and that it may enlarge, it first lessens. (This process) indeed, renders back to us richer and fuller blessings than it deprived us of—by a destruction which is profit, by an injury which is advantage, and by a loss which is gain. In a word, I would say, all creation is instinct with renewal. Whatever you may chance upon, has already existed; whatever you have lost, returns again without fail. All things return to their former state, after having gone out of sight; all things begin after they have ended; they come to an end for the very purpose of coming into existence again. Nothing perishes but with a view to salvation. The whole, therefore, of this revolving order of things bears witness to the resurrection of the dead. In His works did God write it, before He wrote it in the Scriptures; He proclaimed it in His mighty deeds earlier than in His inspired words. He first sent Nature to you as a teacher, meaning to send Prophecy also as a supplemental instructor, that, being Nature's disciple, you may more easily believe Prophecy, and without hesitation accept (its testimony) when you come to hear what you have seen already on every side; nor doubt that God, whom you have discovered to be the restorer of all things, is likewise the reviver of the flesh. And surely, as all things rise again for man, for whose use they have been provided—but not for man except for his flesh also—how happens it that (the flesh) itself can perish utterly, because of which and for the service of which nothing comes to naught?

Chapter XIII. —From Our Author's View of a Verse in the Ninety-Second Psalm, the Phœnix is Made a Symbol of the Resurrection of Our Bodies.

If, however, all nature but faintly figures our resurrection; if creation affords no sign precisely like it, inasmuch as its several phenomena can hardly be said to die so much as to come to an end, nor again be deemed to be reanimated, but only re-formed; then take a most complete and unassailable symbol of our hope, for it shall be an animated being, and subject alike to life and death. I refer to the bird which is peculiar to the East, famous for its singularity, marvelous from its posthumous life, which renews its life in a voluntary death; its dying day is its birthday, for on it it departs and returns; once more a phœnix where just now there was none; once more himself, but just now out of existence; another, yet the same. What can be more express and more significant for our subject; or to what other thing can such a phenomenon bear witness? God even in His own Scripture says: "The righteous shall flourish like the phœnix;" that is, shall flourish or revive, from death, from the grave—to teach you to believe that a bodily substance may be recovered even from the fire. Our Lord has declared that we are "better than many sparrows:" well, if not better than many a phœnix too, it were no great thing. But must men die once for all, while birds in Arabia are sure of a resurrection?

Chapter XIV. —A Sufficient Cause for the Resurrection of the Flesh Occurs in the Future Judgment of Man. It Will Take Cognizance of the Works of the Body No Less Than of the Soul.

Such, then, being the outlines of the divine energies which God has displayed as much in the parables of nature as in His spoken word, let us now approach His very edicts and decrees, since this is the division which we mainly adopt in our subject-matter. We began with the dignity of the flesh, whether it were of such a nature that when once destroyed it was capable of being restored. Then we pursued an inquiry touching the power of God, whether it was sufficiently great to be habitually able to confer this restoration on a thing which had been destroyed. Now, if we have proved these two points, I should like you to inquire into the (question of) cause, whether it be one of sufficient weight to claim the resurrection of the flesh as necessary and as conformable in every way to reason; because there underlies this demurrer: the flesh may be quite capable of being restored, and the Deity be perfectly able to effect the restoration, but a cause for such recovery must needs pre-exist. Admit then a sufficient one, you who learn of a God who is both supremely good as well as just—supremely good from His own (character), just in consequence of ours. For if man had never sinned, he would simply and solely have known God in His superlative goodness, from the attribute of His nature. But now he experiences Him to be a just God also, from the necessity of a cause; still, however, retaining under this very circumstance His excellent goodness, at the same time that He is also just. For, by both succoring the good and punishing the evil, He displays His justice, and at the same time makes both processes contribute proofs of His goodness, whilst on the one hand He deals vengeance, and on the other dispenses reward. But with Marcion you will have the opportunity of more fully learning whether this be the whole character of God. Meanwhile, so perfect is our (God), that He is rightly Judge, because He is the Lord; rightly the Lord, because the Creator; rightly the Creator, because He is God. Whence it happens that that heretic, whose name I know not, holds that He properly is not a Judge, since He is not Lord; properly not Lord, since He is not the Creator. And so I am at a loss to know how He is God, who is neither the Creator, which God is; nor the Lord, which the Creator is. Inasmuch, then, as it is most suitable for the great Being who is God, and Lord, and Creator to summon man to a judgment on this very question, whether he has taken care or not to acknowledge and honor his Lord and Creator, this is just such a judgment as the resurrection shall achieve. The entire cause, then, or rather necessity of the resurrection, will be this, namely, that arrangement of the final judgment which shall be most suitable to God. Now, in effecting this arrangement, you must consider whether the divine censure superintends a judicial examination of the two natures of man—both his soul and his flesh. For that which is a suitable object to be judged, is also a competent one to be raised. Our position is, that the judgment of God must be believed first of all to be plenary, and then absolute, so as to be final, and therefore irrevocable; to be also righteous, not bearing less heavily on any particular part; to be moreover worthy of God, being complete and definite, in keeping with His great patience. Thus it follows that the fullness and perfection of the judgment consists simply in representing the interests of the entire human being. Now, since the entire man consists of the union of the two natures, he must therefore appear in both, as it is right that he should be judged in his entirety; nor, of course, did he pass through life except in his entire state. As therefore he lived, so also must he be judged, because he has to be judged concerning the way in which he lived. For life is the cause of judgment, and it must undergo investigation in as many natures as it possessed when it discharged its vital functions.

Chapter XV. —As the Flesh is a Partaker with the Soul in All Human Conduct, So Will It Be in the Recompense of Eternity.

Come now, let our opponents sever the connection of the flesh with the soul in the affairs of life, that they may be emboldened to sunder it also in the recompense of life. Let them deny their association in acts, that they may be fairly able to deny also their participation in rewards. The flesh ought not to have any share in the sentence, if it had none in the cause of it. Let the soul alone be called back, if it alone went away. But (nothing of the kind ever happened); for the soul alone no more departed from life, than it ran through alone the course from which it departed—I mean this present life. Indeed, the soul alone is so far from conducting (the affairs of) life, that we do not withdraw from community with the flesh even our thoughts, however isolated they be, however unprecipitated into act by means of the flesh; since whatever is done in man's heart is done by the soul in the flesh, and with the flesh, and through the flesh. The Lord Himself, in short, when rebuking our thoughts, includes in His censures this aspect of the flesh, (man's heart), the citadel of the soul: "Why think ye evil in your hearts?" and again: "Whosoever looketh on a woman, to lust after her, hath already committed adultery with her in his heart." So that even the thought, without operation and without effect, is an act of the flesh. But if you allow that the faculty which rules the senses, and which they call Hegemonikon, has its sanctuary in the brain, or in the interval between the eyebrows, or wheresoever the philosophers are pleased to locate it, the flesh will still be the thinking place of the soul. The soul is never without the flesh, as long as it is in the flesh. There is nothing which the flesh does not transact in company with the soul, when without it it does not exist. Consider carefully, too, whether the thoughts are not administered by the flesh, since it is through the flesh that they are distinguished and known externally. Let the soul only meditate some design, the face gives the indication—the face being the mirror of all our intentions. They may deny all combination in acts, but they cannot gainsay their co-operation in thoughts. Still they enumerate the sins of the flesh; surely, then, for its sinful conduct it must be consigned to punishment. But we, moreover, allege against them the virtues of the flesh; surely also for its virtuous conduct it deserves a future reward. Again, as it is the soul which acts and impels us in all we do, so it is the function of the flesh to render obedience. Now we are not permitted to suppose that God is either unjust or idle. Unjust, (however He would be,) were He to exclude from reward the flesh which is associated in good works; and idle, were He to exempt it from punishment, when it has been an accomplice in evil deeds: whereas human judgment is deemed to be the more perfect, when it discovers the agents in every deed, and neither spares the guilty nor grudges the virtuous their full share of either punishment or praise with the principals who employed their services.

Chapter XVI. —The Heretics Called the Flesh "The Vessel of the Soul," In Order to Destroy the Responsibility of the Body. Their Cavil Turns Upon Themselves and Shows the Flesh to Be a Sharer in Human Actions.

When, however, we attribute to the soul authority, and to the flesh submission, we must see to it that (our opponents) do not turn our position by another argument, by insisting on so placing the flesh in the service of the soul, that it be not (considered as) its servant, lest they should be compelled, if it were so regarded, to admit its companionship (to the soul). For they would argue that servants and companions possess a discretion in discharging the functions of their respective office, and a power over their will in both relations: in short, (they would claim to be) men themselves, and therefore (would expect) to share the credit with their principals, to whom they voluntarily yielded their assistance; whereas the flesh had no discretion, no sentiment in itself, but possessing no power of its own of willing or refusing, it, in fact, appears to stand to the soul in the stead of a vessel as an instrument rather than a servant. The soul alone, therefore, will have to be judged (at the last day) preeminently as to how it has employed the vessel of the flesh; the vessel itself, of course, not being amenable to a judicial award: for who condemns the cup if any man has mixed poison in it? or who sentences the sword to the beasts, if a man has perpetrated with it the atrocities of a brigand? Well, now, we will grant that the flesh is innocent, in so far as bad actions will not be charged upon it: what, then, is there to hinder its being saved on the score of its innocence? For although it is free from all imputation of good works, as it is of evil ones, yet it is more consistent with the divine goodness to deliver the innocent. A beneficent man, indeed, is bound to do so: it suits then the character of the Most Bountiful to bestow even gratuitously such a favor. And yet, as to the cup, I will not take the poisoned one, into which some certain death is injected, but one which has been infected with the breath of a lascivious woman, or of Cybele's priest, or of a gladiator, or of a hangman: then I want to know whether you would pass a milder condemnation on it than on the kisses of such persons? One indeed which is soiled with our own filth, or one which is not mingled to our own mind we are apt to dash to pieces, and then to increase our anger with our servant. As for the sword, which is drunk with the blood of the brigand's victims, who would not banish it entirely from his house, much more from his bed-room, or from his pillow, from the presumption that he would be sure to dream of nothing but the apparitions of the souls which were pursuing and disquieting him for lying down with the blade which shed their own blood? Take, however, the cup which has no reproach on it, and which deserves the credit of a faithful ministration, it will be adorned by its drinking-master with chaplets, or be honored with a handful of flowers. The sword also which has received honorable stains in war, and has been thus engaged in a better manslaughter, will secure its own praise by consecration. It is quite possible, then, to pass decisive sentences even on vessels and on instruments, that so they too may participate in the merits of their proprietors and employers. Thus much do I say from a desire to meet even this argument, although there is a failure in the example, owing to the diversity in the nature of the objects. For every vessel or every instrument becomes useful from without, consisting as it does of material perfectly extraneous to the substance of the human owner or employer; whereas the flesh, being conceived, formed, and generated along with the soul from its earliest existence in the womb, is mixed up with it likewise in all its operations. For although it is called "a vessel" by the apostle, such as he enjoins to be treated "with honor," it is yet designated by the same apostle as "the outward man,"—that clay, of course, which at the first was inscribed with the title of a man, not of a cup or a sword, or any paltry vessel. Now it is called a "vessel" in consideration of its capacity, whereby it receives and contains the soul; but "man," from its community of nature, which renders it in all operations a servant and not an instrument. Accordingly, in the judgment it will be held to be a servant (even though it may have no independent discretion of its own), on the ground of its being an integral portion of that which possesses such discretion, and is not a mere chattel. And although the apostle is well aware that the flesh does nothing of itself which is not also imputed to the soul, he yet deems the flesh to be "sinful;" lest it should be supposed to be free from all responsibility by the mere fact of its seeming to be impelled by the soul. So, again, when he is ascribing certain praiseworthy actions to the flesh, he says, "Therefore glorify and exalt God in your body,"—being certain that such efforts are actuated by the soul; but still he ascribes them to the flesh, because it is to it that he also promises the recompense. Besides, neither rebuke, (on the one hand), would have been suitable to it, if free from blame; nor, (on the other hand), would exhortation, if it were incapable of glory. Indeed, both rebuke and exhortation would be alike idle towards the flesh, if it were an improper object for that recompense which is certainly received in the resurrection.

Chapter XVII. —The Flesh Will Be Associated with the Soul in Enduring the Penal Sentences of the Final Judgment.

"Every uneducated person who agrees with our opinion will be apt to suppose that the flesh will have to be present at the final judgment even on this account, because otherwise the soul would be incapable of suffering pain or pleasure, as being incorporeal; for this is the common opinion. We on our part, however, do here maintain, and in a special treatise on the subject prove, that the soul is corporeal, possessing a peculiar kind of solidity in its nature, such as enables it both to perceive and suffer. That souls are even now susceptible of torment and of blessing in Hades, though they are disembodied, and notwithstanding their banishment from the flesh, is proved by the case of Lazarus. I have no doubt given to my opponent room to say: Since, then, the soul has a bodily substance of its own, it will be sufficiently endowed with the faculty of suffering and sense, so as not to require the presence of the flesh. No, no, (is my reply): it will still need the flesh; not as being unable to feel anything without the help of the flesh, but because it is necessary that it should possess such a faculty along with the flesh. For in as far as it has a sufficiency of its own for action, in so far has it likewise a capacity for suffering. But the truth is, in respect of action, it labors under some amount of incapacity; for in its own nature it has simply the ability to think, to will, to desire, to dispose: for fully carrying out the purpose, it looks for the assistance of the flesh. In like manner, it also requires the conjunction of the flesh to endure suffering, in order that by its aid it may be as fully able to suffer, as without its assistance it was not fully able to act. In respect, indeed, of those sins, such as concupiscence, and thought, and wish, which it has a competency of its own to commit, it at once pays the penalty of them. Now, no doubt, if these were alone sufficient to constitute absolute desert without requiring the addition of acts, the soul would suffice in itself to encounter the full responsibility of the judgment, being to be judged for those things in the doing of which it alone had possessed a sufficiency. Since, however, acts too are indissolubly attached to deserts; since also acts are ministerially effected by the flesh, it is no longer enough that the soul apart from the flesh be requited with pleasure or pain for what are actually works of the flesh, although it has a body (of its own), although it has members (of its own), which in like manner are insufficient for its full perception, just as they are also for its perfect action. Therefore, as it has acted in each several instance, so proportionably does it suffer in Hades, being the first to taste of judgment as it was the first to induce to the commission of sin; but still it is waiting for the flesh in order that it may through the flesh also compensate for its deeds, inasmuch as it laid upon the flesh the execution of its own thoughts. This, in short, will be the process of that judgment which is postponed to the last great day, in order that by the exhibition of the flesh the entire course of the divine vengeance may be accomplished. Besides, (it is obvious to remark) there would be no delaying to the end of that doom which souls are already tasting in Hades, if it was destined for souls alone.

Chapter XVIII. —Scripture Phrases and Passages Clearly Assert "The Resurrection of the Dead." The Force of This Very Phrase Explained as Indicating the Prominent Place of the Flesh in the General Resurrection.

Thus far it has been my object by prefatory remarks to lay a foundation for the defense of all the Scriptures which promise a resurrection of the flesh. Now, inasmuch as this verity is supported by so many just and reasonable considerations—I mean the dignity of the flesh itself, the power and might of God, the analogous cases in which these are displayed, as well as the good reasons for the judgment, and the need thereof—it will of course be only right and proper that the Scriptures should be understood in the sense suggested by such authoritative considerations, and not after the conceits of the heretics, which arise from infidelity solely, because it is deemed incredible that the flesh should be recovered from death and restored to life; not because (such a restoration) is either unattainable by the flesh itself, or impossible for God to effect, or unsuitable to the final judgment. Incredible, no doubt, it might be, if it had not been revealed in the word of God; except that, even if it had not been thus first announced by God, it might have been fairly enough assumed, that the revelation of it had been withheld, simply because so many strong presumptions in its favor had been already furnished. Since, however, (the great fact) is proclaimed in so many inspired passages, that is so far a dissuasive against understanding it in a sense different from that which is attested by such arguments as persuade us to its reception, even irrespective of the testimonies of revelation. Let us see, then, first of all in what title this hope of ours is held out to our view. There is, I imagine, one divine edict which is exposed to the gaze of all men: it is "The Resurrection of the Dead." These words are prompt, decisive, clear. I mean to take these very terms, discuss them, and discover to what substance they apply. As to the word resurrection, whenever I hear of its impending over a human being, I am forced to inquire what part of him has been destined to fall, since nothing can be expected to rise again, unless it has first been prostrated. It is only the man who is ignorant of the fact that the flesh falls by death, that can fail to discover that it stands erect by means of life. Nature pronounces God's sentence: "Dust thou art, and unto dust shalt thou return." Even the man who has not heard the sentence, sees the fact. No death but is the ruin of our limbs. This destiny of the body the Lord also described, when, clothed as He was in its very substance, He said, "Destroy this temple, and in three days I will raise it up again." For He showed to what belongs (the incidents of) being destroyed, thrown down, and kept down—even to that to which it also appertains to be lifted and raised up again; although He was at the same time bearing about with Him "a soul that was trembling even unto death," but which did not fall through death, because even the Scripture informs us that "He spoke of His body." So that it is the flesh which falls by death; and accordingly it derives its name, cadaver, from cadendo. The soul, however, has no trace of a fall in its designation, as indeed there is no mortality in its condition. Nay it is the soul which communicates its ruin to the body when it is breathed out of it, just as it is also destined to raise it up again from the earth when it shall re-enter it. That cannot fall which by its entrance raises; nor can that droop which by its departure causes ruin. I will go further, and say that the soul does not even fall into sleep along with the body, nor does it with its companion even lie down in repose. For it is agitated in dreams, and disturbed: it might, however, rest, if it lay down; and lie down it certainly would, if it fell. Thus that which does not fall even into the likeness of death, does not succumb to the reality thereof. Passing now to the other word mortuorum, I wish you to look carefully, and see to what substance it is applicable. Were we to allow, under this head, as is sometimes held by the heretics, that the soul is mortal, so that being mortal it shall attain to a resurrection; this would afford a presumption that the flesh also, being no less mortal, would share in the same resurrection. But our present point is to derive from the proper signification of this word an idea of the destiny which it indicates. Now, just as the term resurrection is predicated of that which falls—that is, the flesh—so will there be the same application of the word dead, because what is called "the resurrection of the dead" indicates the rising up again of that which is fallen down. We learn this from the case of Abraham, the father of the faithful, a man who enjoyed close intercourse with God. For when he requested of the sons of Heth a spot to bury Sarah in, he said to them, "Give me the possession of a burying place with you, that I may bury my dead,"—meaning, of course, her flesh; for he could not have desired a place to bury her soul in, even if the soul is to be deemed mortal, and even if it could bear to be described by the word "dead." Since, then, this word indicates the body, it follows that when "the resurrection of the dead" is spoken of, it is the rising again of men's bodies that is meant.

Chapter XIX. —The Sophistical Sense Put by Heretics on the Phrase "Resurrection of the Dead," As If It Meant the Moral Change of a New Life.

Now this consideration of the phrase in question, and its signification—besides maintaining, of course, the true meaning of the important words—must needs contribute to this further result, that whatever obscurity our adversaries throw over the subject under the presence of figurative and allegorical language, the truth will stand out in clearer light, and out of uncertainties certain and definite rules will be prescribed. For some, when they have alighted on a very usual form of prophetic statement, generally expressed in figure and allegory, though not always, distort into some imaginary sense even the most clearly described doctrine of the resurrection of the dead, alleging that even death itself must be understood in a spiritual sense. They say that which is commonly supposed to be death is not really so—namely, the separation of body and soul: it is rather the ignorance of God, by reason of which man is dead to God, and is not less buried in error than he would be in the grave. Wherefore that also must be held to be the resurrection, when a man is reanimated by access to the truth, and having dispersed the death of ignorance, and being endowed with new life by God, has burst forth from the sepulcher of the old man, even as the Lord likened the scribes and Pharisees to "whited sepulchers." Whence it follows that they who have by faith attained to the resurrection, are with the Lord after they have once put Him on in their baptism. By such subtlety, then, even in conversation have they often been in the habit of misleading our brethren, as if they held a resurrection of the dead as well as we. Woe, say they, to him who has not risen in the present body; for they fear that they might alarm their hearers if they at once denied the resurrection. Secretly, however, in their minds they think this: Woe betide the simpleton who during his present life fails to discover the mysteries of heresy; since this, in their view, is the resurrection. There are however, a great many also, who, claiming to hold a resurrection after the soul's departure, maintain that going out of the sepulcher means escaping out of the world, since in their view the world is the habitation of the dead—that is, of those who know not God; or they will go so far as to say that it actually means escaping out of the body itself, since they imagine that the body detains the soul, when it is shut up in the death of a worldly life, as in a grave.

Chapter XX. —Figurative Senses Have Their Foundation in Literal Fact. Besides, the Allegorical Style is by No Means the Only One Found in the Prophetic Scriptures, as Alleged by the Heretics.

Now, to upset all conceits of this sort, let me dispel at once the preliminary idea on which they rest—their assertion that the prophets make all their announcements in figures of speech. Now, if this were the case, the figures themselves could not possibly have been distinguished, inasmuch as the verities would not have been declared, out of which the figurative language is stretched. And, indeed, if all are figures, where will be that of which they are the figures? How can you hold up a mirror for your face, if the face nowhere exists? But, in truth, all are not figures, but there are also literal statements; nor are all shadows, but there are bodies too: so that we have prophecies about the Lord Himself even, which are clearer than the day. For it was not figuratively that the Virgin conceived in her womb; nor in a trope did she bear Emmanuel, that is, Jesus,

God with us. Even granting that He was figuratively to take the power of Damascus and the spoils of Samaria, still it was literally that He was to "enter into judgment with the elders and princes of the people." For in the person of Pilate "the heathen raged," and in the person of Israel "the people imagined vain things;" "the kings of the earth" in Herod, and the rulers in Annas and Caiaphas, were gathered together "against the Lord, and against His anointed." He, again, was "led as a sheep to the slaughter, and as a sheep before the shearer," that is, Herod, "is dumb, so He opened not His mouth." "He gave His back to scourges, and His cheeks to blows, not turning His face even from the shame of spitting." "He was numbered with the transgressors;" "He was pierced in His hands and His feet;" "they cast lots for his raiment;" "they gave Him gall, and made Him drink vinegar;" "they shook their heads, and mocked Him;" "He was appraised by the traitor in thirty pieces of silver." What figures of speech does Isaiah here give us? What tropes does David? What allegories does Jeremiah? Not even of His mighty works have they used parabolic language. Or else, were not the eyes of the blind opened? did not the tongue of the dumb recover speech? did not the relaxed hands and palsied knees become strong, and the lame leap as an hart? No doubt we are accustomed also to give a spiritual significance to these statements of prophecy, according to the analogy of the physical diseases which were healed by the Lord; but still they were all fulfilled literally: thus showing that the prophets foretold both senses, except that very many of their words can only be taken in a pure and simple signification, and free from all allegorical obscurity; as when we hear of the downfall of nations and cities, of Tyre and Egypt, and Babylon and Edom, and the navy of Carthage; also when they foretell Israel's own chastisements and pardons, its captivities, restorations, and at last its final dispersion. Who would prefer affixing a metaphorical interpretation to all these events, instead of accepting their literal truth? The realities are involved in the words, just as the words are read in the realities. Thus, then, (we find that) the allegorical style is not used in all parts of the prophetic record, although it occasionally occurs in certain portions of it.

Chapter XXI. —No Mere Metaphor in the Phrase Resurrection of the Dead. In Proportion to the Importance of Eternal Truths, is the Clearness of Their Scriptural Enunciation.

Well, if it occurs occasionally in certain portions of it, you will say, then why not in that phrase, where the resurrection might be spiritually understood? There are several reasons why not. First, what must be the meaning of so many important passages of Holy Scripture, which so obviously attest the resurrection of the body, as to admit not even the appearance of a figurative signification? And, indeed, (since some passages are more obscure than others), it cannot but be right—as we have shown above—that uncertain statements should be determined by certain ones, and obscure ones by such as are clear and plain; else there is fear that, in the conflict of certainties and uncertainties, of explicitness and obscurity, faith may be shattered, truth endangered, and the Divine Being Himself be branded as inconstant. Then arises the improbability that the very mystery on which our trust wholly rests, on which also our instruction entirely depends, should have the appearance of being ambiguously announced and obscurely propounded, inasmuch as the hope of the resurrection, unless it be clearly set forth on the sides both of punishment and reward, would fail to persuade any to embrace a religion like ours, exposed as it is to public detestation and the imputation of hostility to others. There is no certain work where the remuneration is uncertain. There is no real apprehension when the peril is only doubtful. But both the recompense of reward, and the danger of losing it, depend on the issues of the resurrection. Now, if even those purposes of God against cities, and nations, and kings, which are merely temporal, local, and personal in their character, have been proclaimed so clearly in prophecy, how is it to be supposed that those dispensations of His which are eternal, and of universal concern to the human race, should be void of all real light in themselves? The grander they are, the clearer should be their announcement, in order that their superior greatness might be believed. And I apprehend that God cannot possibly have ascribed to Him either envy, or guile, or inconsistency, or artifice, by help of which evil qualities it is that all schemes of unusual grandeur are litigiously promulgated.

Chapter XXII. —The Scriptures Forbid Our Supposing Either that the Resurrection is Already Past, or that It Takes Place Immediately at Death. Our Hopes and Prayers Point to the Last Great Day as the Period of Its Accomplishment.

We must after all this turn our attention to those scriptures also which forbid our belief in such a resurrection as is held by your Animalists (for I will not call them Spiritualists), that it is either to be assumed as taking place now, as soon as men come to the knowledge of the truth, or else that it is accomplished immediately after their departure from this life. Now, forasmuch as the seasons of our entire hope have been fixed in the Holy Scripture, and since we are not permitted to place the accomplishment thereof, as I apprehend, previous to Christ's coming, our prayers are directed towards the end of this world, to the passing away thereof at the great day of the Lord—of His wrath and vengeance—the last day, which is hidden (from all), and known to none but the Father, although announced beforehand by signs and wonders, and the dissolution of the elements, and the conflicts of nations. I would turn out the words of the prophets, if the Lord Himself had said nothing (except that prophecies were the Lord's own word); but it is more to my purpose that He by His own mouth confirms their statement. Being questioned by His disciples when those things were to come to pass which He had just been uttering about the destruction of the temple, He discourses to them first of the order of Jewish events until the overthrow of Jerusalem, and then of such as concerned all nations up to the very end of the world. For after He had declared that "Jerusalem was to be trodden down of the Gentiles, until the times of the Gentiles should be fulfilled,"—meaning, of course, those which were to be chosen of God, and gathered in with the remnant of Israel— He then goes on to proclaim, against this world and dispensation (even as Joel had done, and Daniel, and all the prophets with one consent), that "there should be signs in the sun, and in the moon, and in the stars, distress of nations with perplexity, the sea and the waves roaring, men's hearts failing them for fear, and for looking after those things which are coming on the earth." "For," says He, "the powers of heaven shall be shaken; and then shall they see the Son of man coming in the clouds, with power and great glory. And when these things begin to come to pass, then look up, and lift up your heads, for your redemption draweth nigh." He spoke of its "drawing nigh," not of its being present already; and of "those things beginning to come to pass," not of their having happened: because when they have come to pass, then our redemption shall be at hand, which is said to be approaching up to that time, raising and exciting our minds to what is then the proximate harvest of our hope. He immediately annexes a parable of this in "the trees which are tenderly sprouting into a flower-stalk, and then developing the flower, which is the precursor of the fruit." "So likewise ye," (He adds), "when ye shall see all these things come to pass, know ye that the kingdom of heaven is nigh at hand." "Watch ye, therefore, and pray always, that ye may be accounted worthy to escape all those things, and to stand before the Son of man;" that is, no doubt, at the resurrection, after all these things have been previously transacted. Therefore, although there is a sprouting in the acknowledgment of all this mystery, yet it is only in the actual presence of the Lord that the flower is developed and the fruit borne. Who is it then, that has aroused the Lord, now at God's right hand, so unseasonably and with such severity "shake terribly" (as Isaiah expresses it) "that earth," which, I suppose, is as yet unshattered? Who has thus early put "Christ's enemies beneath His feet" (to use the language of David), making Him more hurried than the Father, whilst every crowd in our popular assemblies is still with shouts consigning "the Christians to the lions?" Who has yet beheld Jesus descending from heaven in like manner as the apostles saw Him ascend, according to the appointment of the two angels? Up to the present moment they have not, tribe by tribe, smitten their breasts, looking on Him whom they pierced. No one has as yet fallen in with Elias; no one has as yet escaped from Antichrist; no one has as yet had to bewail the downfall of Babylon. And is there now anybody who has risen again, except the heretic? He, of course, has already quitted the grave of his own corpse—although he is even now liable to fevers and ulcers; he, too, has already trodden down his enemies—although he has even now to struggle with the powers of the world. And as a matter of course, he is already a king—although he even now owes to Cæsar the things which are Cæsar's.

Chapter XXIII. —Sundry Passages of St. Paul, Which Speak of a Spiritual Resurrection, Compatible with the Future Resurrection of the Body, Which is Even Assumed in Them.

The apostle indeed teaches, in his Epistle to the Colossians, that we were once dead, alienated, and enemies to the Lord in our minds, whilst we were living in wicked works; that we were then buried with Christ in baptism, and also raised again with Him through the faith of the operation of God, who hath raised Him from the dead. "And you, (adds he), when ye were dead in sins and the uncircumcision of your flesh, hath He quickened together with Him, having forgiven you all trespasses." And again: "If ye are dead with Christ from the elements of the world, why, as though living in the world, are ye subject to ordinances?" Now, since he makes us spiritually dead—in such a way, however, as to allow that we shall one day have to undergo a bodily death—so, considering indeed that we have been also raised in a like spiritual sense, he equally allows that we shall further have to undergo a bodily resurrection. In so many words he says: "Since ye are risen with Christ, seek those things which are above, where Christ sitteth at the right hand of God. Set your affection on things above, not on things on the earth." Accordingly, it is in our mind that he shows that we rise (with Christ), since it is by this alone that we are as yet able to reach to heavenly objects. These we should not "seek," nor "set our affection on," if we had them already in our possession. He also adds: "For ye are dead"—to your sins, he means, not to yourselves—"and your life is hid with Christ in God." Now that life is not yet apprehended which is hidden. In like manner John says: "And it doth not yet appear what we shall be: we know, however, that when He shall be manifest, we shall be like Him." We are far indeed from being already what we know not of; we should, of course, be sure to know it if we were already (like Him). It is therefore the contemplation of our blessed hope even in this life by faith (that he speaks of)—not its presence nor its possession, but only its expectation. Concerning this expectation and hope Paul writes to the Galatians: "For we through the Spirit wait for the hope of righteousness by faith." He says "we wait for it," not we are in possession of it. By the righteousness of God, he means that judgment which we shall have to undergo as the recompense of our deeds. It is in expectation of this for himself that the apostle writes to the Philippians: "If by any means," says he, "I might attain to the resurrection of the dead. Not as though I had already attained, or were already perfect." And yet he had believed, and had known all mysteries, as an elect vessel and the great teacher of the Gentiles; but for all that he goes on to say: "I, however, follow on, if so be I may apprehend that for which I also am apprehended of Christ." Nay, more: "Brethren," (he adds), "I count not myself to have apprehended: but this one thing (I do), forgetting those things which are behind, and reaching forth unto those things which are before, I press toward the mark for the prize of blamelessness, whereby I may attain it;" meaning the resurrection from the dead in its proper time. Even as he says to the Galatians: "Let us not be weary in well-doing: for in due season we shall reap." Similarly, concerning Onesiphorus, does he also write to Timothy: "The Lord grant unto him that he may find mercy in that day;" unto which day and time he charges Timothy himself "to keep what had been committed to his care, without spot, unrebukable, until the appearing of the Lord Jesus Christ: which in His times He shall show, who is the blessed and only Potentate, the King of kings and Lord of lords," speaking of (Him as) God. It is to these same times that Peter in the Acts refers, when he says: "Repent ye therefore, and be converted, that your sins may be blotted out, when the times of refreshing shall come from the presence of the Lord; and He shall send Jesus Christ, which before was preached unto you: whom the heaven must receive until the times of restitution of all things, which God hath spoken by the mouth of His holy prophets."

Chapter XXIV. —Other Passages Quoted from St. Paul, Which Categorically Assert the Resurrection of the Flesh at the Final Judgment.

The character of these times learn, along with the Thessalonians. For we read: "How ye turned from idols to serve the living and true God, and to wait for His Son from heaven, whom He raised from the dead, even Jesus." And again: "For what is our hope, or joy, or crown of rejoicing? Are not even ye in the presence of our Lord God, Jesus Christ, at His coming?" Likewise: "Before God, even our Father, at the coming of the Lord Jesus Christ, with the whole company of His saints." He teaches them that they must "not sorrow concerning them that are asleep," and at the same time explains to them the times of the resurrection, saying, "For if we believe that Jesus died and rose again, even so them also which sleep in Jesus shall God bring with Him. For this we say unto you by the word of the Lord, that we which are alive and remain unto the coming of our Lord, shall not prevent them that are asleep. For the Lord Himself shall descend from heaven with a shout, with the voice of the archangel, and with the trump of God; and the dead in Christ shall rise first: then we which are alive and remain shall be caught up together with them in the clouds, to meet the Lord in the air; and so shall we be ever with the Lord." What archangel's voice, (I wonder), what trump of God is now heard, except it be, forsooth, in the entertainments of the heretics? For, allowing that the word of the gospel may be called "the trump of God," since it was still calling men, yet they must at that time either be dead as to the body, that they may be able to rise again; and then how are they alive? Or else caught up into the clouds; and how then are they here? "Most miserable," no doubt, as the apostle declared them, are they "who in this life only" shall be found to have hope: they will have to be excluded while they are with premature haste seizing that which is promised after this life; erring concerning the truth, no less than Phygellus and Hermogenes. Hence it is that the Holy Ghost, in His greatness, foreseeing clearly all such interpretations as these, suggests (to the apostle), in this very epistle of his to the Thessalonians, as follows: "But of the times and the seasons, brethren, there is no necessity for my writing unto you. For ye yourselves know perfectly, that the day of the Lord cometh as a thief in the night. For when they shall say, 'Peace,' and 'All things are safe,' then sudden destruction shall come upon them." Again, in the second epistle he addresses them with even greater earnestness: "Now I beseech you, brethren, by the coming of our Lord Jesus Christ, and by our gathering together unto Him, that ye be not soon shaken in mind, nor be troubled, either by spirit, or by word," that is, the word of false prophets, "or by letter," that is, the letter of false apostles, "as if from us, as that the day of the Lord is at hand. Let no man deceive you by any means. For that day shall not come, unless indeed there first come a falling away," he means indeed of this present empire, "and that man of sin be revealed," that is to say, Antichrist, "the son of perdition, who opposeth and exalteth himself above all that is called God or religion; so that he sitteth in the temple of God, affirming that he is God. Remember ye not, that when I was with you, I used to tell you these things? And now ye know what detaineth, that he might be revealed in his time. For the mystery of iniquity doth already work; only he who now hinders must hinder, until he be taken out of the way." What obstacle is there but the Roman state, the falling away of which, by being scattered into ten kingdoms, shall introduce Antichrist upon (its own ruins)? "And then shall be revealed the wicked one, whom the Lord shall consume with the spirit of His mouth, and shall destroy with the brightness of His coming: even him whose coming is after the working of Satan, with all power, and signs, and lying wonders, and with all deceivableness of unrighteousness in them that perish."

Chapter XXV.—St. John, in the Apocalypse, Equally Explicit in Asserting the Same Great Doctrine.

In the Revelation of John, again, the order of these times is spread out to view, which "the souls of the martyrs" are taught to wait for beneath the altar, whilst they earnestly pray to be avenged and judged: (taught, I say, to wait), in order that the world may first drink to the dregs the plagues that await it out of the vials of the angels, and that the city of fornication may receive from the ten kings its deserved doom, and that the beast Antichrist with his false prophet may wage war on the Church of God; and that, after the casting of the devil into the bottomless pit for a while, the blessed prerogative of the first resurrection may be ordained from the thrones; and then again, after the consignment of him to the fire, that the judgment of the final and universal resurrection may be determined out of the books. Since, then, the Scriptures both indicate the stages of the last times, and concentrate the harvest of the Christian hope in the very end of the world, it is evident, either that all which God promises to us receives its accomplishment then, and thus what the heretics pretend about a resurrection here falls to the ground; or else, even allowing that a confession of the mystery (of divine truth) is a resurrection, that there is, without any detriment to this view, room for believing in that which is announced for the end. It moreover follows, that the very maintenance of this spiritual resurrection amounts to a presumption in favor of the other bodily resurrection; for if none were announced for that time, there would be fair ground for asserting only this purely spiritual resurrection. Inasmuch, however, as (a resurrection) is proclaimed for the last time, it is proved to be a bodily one, because there is no spiritual one also then announced. For why make a second announcement of a resurrection of only one character, that is, the spiritual one, since this ought to be undergoing accomplishment either now, without any regard to different times, or else then, at the very conclusion of all the periods? It is therefore more competent for us even to maintain a spiritual resurrection at the commencement of a life of faith, who acknowledge the full completion thereof at the end of the world.

Chapter XXVI. —Even the Metaphorical Descriptions of This Subject in the Scriptures Point to the Bodily Resurrection, the Only Sense Which Secures Their Consistency and Dignity.

To a preceding objection, that the Scriptures are allegorical, I have still one answer to make—that it is open to us also to defend the bodily character of the resurrection by means of the language of the prophets, which is equally figurative. For consider that primeval sentence which God spoke when He called man earth; saying, "Earth thou art, and to earth shalt thou return." In respect, of course, to his fleshly substance, which had been taken out of the ground, and which was the first to receive the name of man, as we have already shown, does not this passage give one instruction to interpret in relation to the flesh also whatever of wrath or of grace God has determined for the earth, because, strictly speaking, the earth is not exposed to His judgment, since it has never done any good or evil? "Cursed," no doubt, it was, for it drank the blood of man; but even this was as a figure of homicidal flesh. For if the earth has to suffer either joy or injury, it is simply on man's account, that he may suffer the joy or the sorrow through the events which happen to his dwelling-place, whereby he will rather have to pay the penalty which, simply on his account, even the earth must suffer. When, therefore, God even threatens the earth, I would prefer saying that He threatens the flesh: so likewise, when He makes a promise to the earth, I would rather understand Him as promising the flesh; as in that passage of David: "The Lord is King, let the earth be glad,"— meaning the flesh of the saints, to which appertains the enjoyment of the kingdom of God. Then he afterwards says: "The earth saw and trembled; the mountains melted like wax at the presence of the Lord,"—meaning, no doubt the flesh of the wicked; and (in a similar sense) it is written: "For they shall look on Him whom they pierced." If indeed it will be thought that both these passages were pronounced simply of the element earth, how can it be consistent that it should shake and melt at the presence of the Lord, at whose royal dignity it before exulted? So again in Isaiah, "Ye shall eat the good of the land," the expression means the blessings which await the flesh when in the kingdom of God it shall be renewed, and made like the angels, and waiting to obtain the things "which neither eye hath seen, nor ear heard, and which have not entered into the heart of man." Otherwise, how vain that God should invite men to obedience by the fruits of the field and the elements of this life, when He dispenses these to even irreligious men and blasphemers; on a general condition once for all made to man, "sending rain on the good and on the evil, and making His sun to shine on the just and on the unjust!" Happy, no doubt, is faith, if it is to obtain gifts which the enemies of God and Christ not only use, but even abuse, "worshipping the creature itself in opposition to the Creator!" You will reckon, (I suppose) onions and truffles among earth's bounties, since the Lord declares that "man shall not live on bread alone!" In this way the Jews lose heavenly blessings, by confining their hopes to earthly ones, being ignorant of the promise of heavenly bread, and of the oil of God's unction, and the wine of the Spirit, and of that water of life which has its vigor from the vine of Christ. On exactly the same principle, they consider the special soil of Judea to be that very holy land, which ought rather to be interpreted of the Lord's flesh, which, in all those who put on Christ, is thenceforward the holy land; holy indeed by the indwelling of the Holy Ghost, truly flowing with milk and honey by the sweetness of His assurance, truly Judean by reason of the friendship of God. For "he is not a Jew which is one outwardly, but he who is one inwardly." In the same way it is that both God's temple and Jerusalem (must be understood) when it is said by Isaiah: "Awake, awake, O Jerusalem! put on the strength of thine arm; awake, as in thine earliest time," that is to say, in that innocence which preceded the fall into sin. For how can words of this kind of exhortation and invitation be suitable for that Jerusalem which killed the prophets, and stoned those that were sent to them, and at last crucified its very Lord? Neither indeed is salvation promised to any one land at all, which must needs pass away with the fashion of the whole world. Even if anybody should venture strongly to contend that paradise is the holy land, which it may be possible to designate as the land of our first parents Adam and Eve, it will even then follow that the restoration of paradise will seem to be promised to the flesh, whose lot it was to inhabit and keep it, in order that man may be recalled thereto just such as he was driven from it.

Chapter XXVII. —Certain Metaphorical Terms Explained of the Resurrection of the Flesh.

We have also in the Scriptures robes mentioned as allegorizing the hope of the flesh. Thus in the Revelation of John it is said: "These are they which have not defiled their clothes with women,"—indicating, of course, virgins, and such as have become "eunuchs for the kingdom of heaven's sake." Therefore, they shall be "clothed in white raiment," that is, in the bright beauty of the unwedded flesh. In the gospel even, "the wedding garment" may be regarded as the sanctity of the flesh. And so, when Isaiah tells us what sort of "fast the Lord hath chosen," and subjoins a statement about the reward of good works, he says: "Then shall thy light break forth as the morning, and thy garments, shall speedily arise;" where he has no thought of cloaks or stuff gowns, but means the rising of the flesh, which he declared the resurrection of, after its fall in death. Thus we are furnished even with an allegorical defense of the resurrection of the body. When, then, we read, "Go, my people, enter into your closets for a little season, until my anger pass away," we have in the closets graves, in which they will have to rest for a little while, who shall have at the end of the world departed this life in the last furious onset of the power of Antichrist. Why else did He use the expression closets, in preference to some other receptacle, if it were not that the flesh is kept in these closets or cellars salted and reserved for use, to be drawn out thence on a suitable occasion? It is on a like principle that embalmed corpses are set aside for burial in mausoleums and sepulchers, in order that they may be removed therefrom when the Master shall order it. Since, therefore, there is consistency in thus understanding the passage (for what refuge of little closets could possibly shelter us from the wrath of God?), it appears that by the very phrase which he uses, "Until His anger pass away," which shall extinguish Antichrist, he in fact shows that after that indignation the flesh will come forth from the sepulcher, in which it had been deposited previous to the bursting out of the anger. Now out of the closets nothing else is brought than that which had been put into them, and after the extirpation of Antichrist shall be busily transacted the great process of the resurrection.

Chapter XXVIII. —Prophetic Things and Actions, as Well as Words, Attest This Great Doctrine.

But we know that prophecy expressed itself by things no less than by words. By words, and also by deeds, is the resurrection foretold. When Moses puts his hand into his bosom, and then draws it out again dead, and again puts his hand into his bosom, and plucks it out living, does not this apply as a presage to all mankind?—inasmuch as those three signs denoted the threefold power of God: when it shall, first, in the appointed order, subdue to man the old serpent, the devil, however formidable; then, secondly, draw forth the flesh from the bosom of death; and then, at last, shall pursue all blood (shed) in judgment. On this subject we read in the writings of the same prophet, (how that) God says: "For your blood of your lives will I require of all wild beasts; and I will require it of the hand of man, and of his brother's hand." Now nothing is required except that which is demanded back again, and nothing is thus demanded except that which is to be given up; and that will of course be given up, which shall be demanded and required on the ground of vengeance. But indeed there cannot possibly be punishment of that which never had any existence. Existence, however, it will have, when it is restored in order to be punished. To the flesh, therefore, applies everything which is declared respecting the blood, for without the flesh there cannot be blood. The flesh will be raised up in order that the blood may be punished. There are, again, some statements (of Scripture) so plainly made as to be free from all obscurity of allegory, and yet they strongly require their very simplicity to be interpreted. There is, for instance, that passage in Isaiah: "I will kill, and I will make alive." Certainly His making alive is to take place after He has killed. As, therefore, it is by death that He kills, it is by the resurrection that He will make alive. Now it is the flesh which is killed by death; the flesh, therefore, will be revived by the resurrection. Surely if killing means taking away life from the flesh, and its opposite, reviving, amounts to restoring life to the flesh, it must needs be that the flesh rise again, to which the life, which has been taken away by killing, has to be restored by vivification.

Chapter XXIX. —Ezekiel's Vision of the Dry Bones Quoted.

Inasmuch, then, as even the figurative portions of Scripture, and the arguments of facts, and some plain statements of Holy Writ, throw light upon the resurrection of the flesh (although without specially naming the very substance), how much more effectual for determining the question will not those passages be which indicate the actual substance of the body by expressly mentioning it! Take Ezekiel: "And the hand of the Lord," says he, "was upon me; and the Lord brought me forth in the Spirit, and set me in the midst of a plain which was full of bones; and He led me round about them in a circuit: and, behold, there were many on the face of the plain; and, lo, they were very dry. And He said unto me, Son of man, will these bones live? And I said, O Lord God, Thou knowest. And He said unto me, Prophesy upon these bones; and thou shalt say, Ye dry bones, hear the word of the Lord. Thus saith the Lord God to these bones, Behold, I bring upon you the breath of life, and ye shall live: and I will give unto you the spirit, and I will place muscles over you, and I will spread skin upon you; and ye shall live, and shall know that I am the Lord. And I prophesied as the Lord commanded me: and while I prophesy, behold there is a voice, behold also a movement, and bones approached bones. And I saw, and behold sinews and flesh came up over them, and muscles were placed around them; but there was no breath in them. And He said unto me, Prophesy to the wind, son of man, prophesy and say, Thus saith the Lord God, Come from the four winds, O breath, and breathe in these dead men, and let them live. So I prophesied to the wind, as He commanded me, and the spirit entered into the bones, and they lived, and stood upon their feet, strong and exceeding many. And the Lord said unto me, Son of man, these bones are the whole house of Israel. They say themselves, Our bones are become dry, and our hope is perished, and we in them have been violently destroyed. Therefore, prophesy unto them, (and say), Behold, even I will open your sepulchers, and will bring you out of your sepulchers, O my people, and will bring you into the land of Israel: and ye shall know how that I the Lord opened your sepulchers, and brought you, O my people, out of your sepulchers; and I will give my Spirit unto you, and ye shall live, and shall rest in your own land: and ye shall know how that I the Lord have spoken and done these things, saith the Lord."

Chapter XXX. —This Vision Interpreted by Tertullian of the Resurrection of the Bodies of the Dead. A Chronological Error of Our Author, Who Supposes that Ezekiel in His Ch. XXXI. Prophesied Before the Captivity.

I am well aware how they torture even this prophecy into a proof of the allegorical sense, on the ground that by saying, "These bones are the whole house of Israel," He made them a figure of Israel, and removed them from their proper literal condition; and therefore (they contend) that there is here a figurative, not a true prediction of the resurrection, for (they say) the state of the Jews is one of humiliation, in a certain sense dead, and very dry, and dispersed over the plain of the world. Therefore the image of a resurrection is allegorically applied to their state, since it has to be gathered together, and recompacted bone to bone (in other words, tribe to tribe, and people to people), and to be reincorporated by the sinews of power and the nerves of royalty, and to be brought out as it were from sepulchers, that is to say, from the most miserable and degraded abodes of captivity, and to breathe afresh in the way of a restoration, and to live thenceforward in their own land of Judea. And what is to happen after all this? They will die, no doubt. And what will there be after death? No resurrection from the dead, of course, since there is nothing of the sort here revealed to Ezekiel. Well, but the resurrection is elsewhere foretold: so that there will be one even in this case, and they are rash in applying this passage to the state of Jewish affairs; or even if it do indicate a different recovery from the resurrection which we are maintaining, what matters it to me, provided there be also a resurrection of the body, just as there is a restoration of the Jewish state? In fact, by the very circumstance that the recovery of the Jewish state is prefigured by the reincorporation and reunion of bones, proof is offered that this event will also happen to the bones themselves; for the metaphor could not have been formed from bones, if the same thing exactly were not to be realized in them also. Now, although there is a sketch of the true thing in its image, the image itself still possesses a truth of its own: it must needs be, therefore, that must have a prior existence for itself, which is used figuratively to express some other thing. Vacuity is not a consistent basis for a similitude, nor does nonentity form a suitable foundation for a parable. It will therefore be right to believe that the bones are destined to have a rehabiliment of flesh and breath, such as it is here said they will have, by reason indeed of which their renewed state could alone express the reformed condition of Jewish affairs, which is pretended to be the meaning of this passage. It is, however, more characteristic of a religious spirit to maintain the truth on the authority of a literal interpretation, such as is required by the sense of the inspired passage. Now, if this vision had reference to the condition of the Jews, as soon as He had revealed to him the position of the bones, He would at once have added, "These bones are the whole house of Israel," and so forth. But immediately on showing the bones, He interrupts the scene by saying somewhat of the prospect which is most suited to bones; without yet naming Israel, He tries the prophet's own faith: "Son of man, can these bones ever live?" so that he makes answer: "O Lord, Thou knowest." Now God would not, you may be sure, have tried the prophet's faith on a point which was never to be a real one, of which Israel should never hear, and in which it was not proper to repose belief. Since, however, the resurrection of the dead was indeed foretold, but Israel, in the distrust of his great unbelief, was offended at it; and, whilst gazing on the condition of the crumbling grave, despaired of a resurrection; or rather, did not direct his mind mainly to it, but to his own harassing circumstances,— therefore God first instructed the prophet (since he, too, was not free from doubt), by revealing to him the process of the resurrection, with a view to his earnest setting forth of the same. He then charged the people to believe what He had revealed to the prophet, telling them that they were themselves, though refusing to believe their resurrection, the very bones which were destined to rise again. Then in the concluding sentence He says, "And ye shall know how that I the Lord have spoken and done these things," intending of course to do that of which He had spoken; but certainly not meaning to do that which He had spoken of, if His design had been to do something different from what He had said.

Chapter XXXI. —Other Passages Out of the Prophets Applied to the Resurrection of the Flesh.

Unquestionably, if the people were indulging in figurative murmurs that their bones were become dry, and that their hope had perished—plaintive at the consequences of their dispersion—then God might fairly enough seem to have consoled their figurative despair with a figurative promise. Since, however, no injury had as yet alighted on the people from their dispersion, although the hope of the resurrection had very frequently failed amongst them, it is manifest that it was owing to the perishing condition of their bodies that their faith in the resurrection was shaken. God, therefore, was rebuilding the faith which the people were pulling down. But even if it were true that Israel was then depressed at some shock in their existing circumstances, we must not on that account suppose that the purpose of revelation could have rested in a parable: its aim must have been to testify a resurrection, in order to raise the nation's hope to even an eternal salvation and an indispensable restoration, and thereby turn off their minds from brooding over their present affairs. This indeed is the aim of other prophets likewise. "Ye shall go forth," (says Malachi), "from your sepulchers, as young calves let loose from their bonds, and ye shall tread down your enemies." And again, (Isaiah says): "Your heart shall rejoice, and your bones shall spring up like the grass," because the grass also is renewed by the dissolution and corruption of the seed. In a word, if it is contended that the figure of the rising bones refers properly to the state of Israel, why is the same hope announced to all nations, instead of being limited to Israel only, of reinvesting those osseous remains with bodily substance and vital breath, and of raising up their dead out of the grave? For the language is universal: "The dead shall arise, and come forth from their graves; for the dew which cometh from Thee is medicine to their bones." In another passage it is written: "All flesh shall come to worship before me, saith the Lord." When? When the fashion of this world shall begin to pass away. For He said before: "As the new heaven and the new earth, which I make, remain before me, saith the Lord, so shall your seed remain." Then also shall be fulfilled what is written afterwards: "And they shall go forth" (namely, from their graves), "and shall see the carcasses of those who have transgressed: for their worm shall never die, nor shall their fire be quenched; and they shall be a spectacle to all flesh" even to that which, being raised again from the dead and brought out from the grave, shall adore the Lord for this great grace.

Chapter XXXII. —Even Unburied Bodies Will Be Raised Again. Whatever Befalls Them God Will Restore Them Again. Jonah's Case Quoted in Illustration of God's Power.

But, that you may not suppose that it is merely those bodies which are consigned to tombs whose resurrection is foretold, you have it declared in Scripture: "And I will command the fishes of the sea, and they shall cast up the bones which they have devoured; and I will bring joint to joint, and bone to bone." You will ask, Will then the fishes and other animals and carnivorous birds be raised again, in order that they may vomit up what they have consumed, on the ground of your reading in the law of Moses, that blood is required of even all the beasts? Certainly not. But the beasts and the fishes are mentioned in relation to the restoration of flesh and blood, in order the more emphatically to express the resurrection of such bodies as have even been devoured, when redress is said to be demanded of their very devourers. Now I apprehend that in the case of Jonah we have a fair proof of this divine power, when he comes forth from the fish's belly uninjured in both his natures—his flesh and his soul. No doubt the bowels of the whale would have had abundant time during three days for consuming and digesting Jonah's flesh, quite as effectually as a coffin, or a tomb, or the gradual decay of some quiet and concealed grave; only that he wanted to prefigure even those beasts (which symbolize) especially the men who are wildly opposed to the Christian name, or the angels of iniquity, of whom blood will be required by the full exaction of an avenging judgment. Where, then, is the man who, being more disposed to learn than to assume, more careful to believe than to dispute, and more scrupulous of the wisdom of God than wantonly bent on his own, when he hears of a divine purpose respecting sinews and skin, and nerves and bones, will forthwith devise some different application of these words, as if all that is said of the substances in question were not naturally intended for man? For either there is here no reference to the destiny of man—in the gracious provision of the kingdom (of heaven), in the severity of the judgment-day, in all the incidents of the resurrection; or else, if there is any reference to his destiny, the destination must necessarily be made in reference to those substances of which the man is composed, for whom the destiny is reserved. Another question I have also to ask of these very adroit transformers of bones and sinews, and nerves and sepulchers: Why, when anything is declared of the soul, do they not interpret the soul to be something else, and transfer it to another signification?—since, whenever any distinct statement is made of a bodily substance, they will obstinately prefer taking any other sense whatever, rather than that which the name indicates. If things which pertain to the body are figurative, why are not those which pertain to the soul figurative also? Since, however, things which belong to the soul have nothing allegorical in them, neither therefore have those which belong to the body. For man is as much body as he is soul; so that it is impossible for one of these natures to admit a figurative sense, and the other to exclude it.

Chapter XXXIII—So Much for the Prophetic Scriptures. In the Gospels, Christ's Parables, as Explained by Himself, Have a Clear Reference to the Resurrection of the Flesh.

This is evidence enough from the prophetic Scriptures. I now appeal to the Gospels. But here also I must first meet the same sophistry as advanced by those who contend that the Lord, like (the prophets), said everything in the way of allegory, because it is written: "All these things spoke Jesus in parables, and without a parable spoke He not unto them," that is, to the Jews. Now the disciples also asked Him, "Why speakest Thou in parables?" And the Lord gave them this answer: "Therefore I speak unto them in parables: because they seeing, see not; and hearing, they hear not, according to the prophecy of Esaias." But since it was to the Jews that He spoke in parables, it was not then to all men; and if not to all, it follows that it was not always and in all things parables with Him, but only in certain things, and when addressing a particular class. But He addressed a particular class when He spoke to the Jews. It is true that He spoke sometimes even to the disciples in parables. But observe how the Scripture relates such a fact: "And He spoke a parable unto them." It follows, then, that He did not usually address them in parables; because if He always did so, special mention would not be made of His resorting to this mode of address. Besides, there is not a parable which you will not find to be either explained by the Lord Himself, as that of the sower, (which He interprets) of the management of the word of God; or else cleared by a preface from the writer of the Gospel, as in the parable of the arrogant judge and the importunate widow, which is expressly applied to earnestness in prayer; or capable of being spontaneously understood, as in the parable of the fig-tree, which was spared a while in hopes of improvement—an emblem of Jewish sterility. Now, if even parables obscure not the light of the gospel, how unlikely it is that plain sentences and declarations, which have an unmistakeable meaning, should signify any other thing than their literal sense! But it is by such declarations and sentences that the Lord sets forth either the last judgment, or the kingdom, or the resurrection: "It shall be more tolerable," He says, "for Tyre and Sidon in the day of judgment than for you." And "Tell them that the kingdom of God is at hand." And again, "It shall be recompensed to you at the resurrection of the just." Now, if the mention of these events (I mean the judgment-day, and the kingdom of God, and the resurrection) has a plain and absolute sense, so that nothing about them can be pressed into an allegory, neither should those statements be forced into parables which describe the arrangement, and the process, and the experience of the kingdom of God, and of the judgment, and of the resurrection. On the contrary, things which are destined for the body should be carefully understood in a bodily sense—not in a spiritual sense, as having nothing figurative in their nature. This is the reason why we have laid it down as a preliminary consideration, that the bodily substance both of the soul and of the flesh is liable to the recompense, which will have to be awarded in return for the co-operation of the two natures, that so the corporeality of the soul may not exclude the bodily nature of the flesh by suggesting a recourse to figurative descriptions, since both of them must needs be regarded as destined to take part in the kingdom, and the judgment, and the resurrection. And now we proceed to the special proof of this proposition, that the bodily character of the flesh is indicated by our Lord whenever He mentions the resurrection, at the same time without disparagement to the corporeal nature of the soul—a point which has been actually admitted but by a few.

Chapter XXXIV—Christ Plainly Testifies to the Resurrection of the Entire Man. Not in His Soul Only, Without the Body.

To begin with the passage where He says that He is come to "to seek and to save that which is lost." What do you suppose that to be which is lost? Man, undoubtedly. The entire man, or only a part of him? The whole man, of course. In fact, since the transgression which caused man's ruin was committed quite as much by the instigation of the soul from concupiscence as by the action of the flesh from actual fruition, it has marked the entire man with the sentence of transgression, and has therefore made him deservedly amenable to perdition. So that he will be wholly saved, since he has by sinning been wholly lost. Unless it be true that the sheep (of the parable) is a "lost" one, irrespective of its body; then its recovery may be effected without the body. Since, however, it is the bodily substance as well as the soul, making up the entire animal, which was carried on the shoulders of the Good Shepherd, we have here unquestionably an example how man is restored in both his natures. Else how unworthy it were of God to bring only a moiety of man to salvation—and almost less than that; whereas the munificence of princes of this world always claims for itself the merit of a plenary grace! Then must the devil be understood to be stronger for injuring man, ruining him wholly? and must God have the character of comparative weakness, since He does not relieve and help man in his entire state? The apostle, however, suggests that "where sin abounded, there has grace much more abounded." How, in fact, can he be regarded as saved, who can at the same time be said to be lost—lost, that is, in the flesh, but saved as to his soul? Unless, indeed, their argument now makes it necessary that the soul should be placed in a "lost" condition, that it may be susceptible of salvation, on the ground that is properly saved which has been lost. We, however, so understand the soul's immortality as to believe it "lost," not in the sense of destruction, but of punishment, that is, in hell. And if this is the case, then it is not the soul which salvation will affect, since it is "safe" already in its own nature by reason of its immortality, but rather the flesh, which, as all readily allow, is subject to destruction. Else, if the soul is also perishable (in this sense), in other words, not immortal—the condition of the flesh—then this same condition ought in all fairness to benefit the flesh also, as being similarly mortal and perishable, since that which perishes the Lord purposes to save. I do not care now to follow the clue of our discussion, so far as to consider whether it is in one of his natures or in the other that perdition puts in its claim on man, provided that salvation is equally distributed over the two substances, and makes him its aim in respect of them both. For observe, in which substance so-ever you assume man to have perished, in the other he does not perish. He will therefore be saved in the substance in which he does not perish, and yet obtain salvation in that in which he does perish. You have (then) the restoration of the entire man, inasmuch as the Lord purposes to save that part of him which perishes, whilst he will not of course lose that portion which cannot be lost. Who will any longer doubt of the safety of both natures, when one of them is to obtain salvation, and the other is not to lose it? And, still further, the Lord explains to us the meaning of the thing when He says: "I came not to do my own will, but the Father's, who hath sent me." What, I ask, is that will? "That of all which He hath given me I should lose nothing, but should raise it up again at the last day." Now, what had Christ received of the Father but that which He had Himself put on? Man, of course, in his texture of flesh and soul. Neither, therefore, of those parts which He has received will He allow to perish; nay, no considerable portion—nay, not the least fraction, of either. If the flesh be, as our opponents slightingly think, but a poor fraction, then the flesh is safe, because not a fraction of man is to perish; and no larger portion is in danger, because every portion of man is in equally safe keeping with Him. If, however, He will not raise the flesh also up at the last day, then He will permit not only a fraction of man to perish, but (as I will venture to say, in consideration of so important a part) almost the whole of him. But when He repeats His words with increased emphasis, "And this is the Father's will, that everyone which seeth the Son, and believeth on Him, may have eternal life: and I will raise him up at the last day,"—He asserts the full extent of the resurrection. For He assigns to each several natures that reward which is suited to its services: both to the flesh, for by it the Son was "seen;" and to the soul, for by it He was "believed on." Then, you will say, to them was this promise given by whom Christ was "seen." Well, be it so; only let the same hope flow on from them to us! For if to them who saw, and therefore believed, such fruit then accrued to the operations of the flesh and the soul, how much more to us! For more "blessed," says Christ, "are they who have not seen, and yet have believed;" since, even if the resurrection of the flesh must be denied to them, it must at any rate be a fitting boon to us, who are the more blessed. For how could we be blessed, if we were to perish in any part of us?

Chapter XXXV. —Explanation of What is Meant by the Body, Which is to Be Raised Again. Not the Corporeality of the Soul.

But He also teaches us, that "He is rather to be feared, who is able to destroy both body and soul in hell," that is, the Lord alone; "not those which kill the body, but are not able to hurt the soul," that is to say, all human powers. Here, then, we have a recognition of the natural immortality of the soul, which cannot be killed by men; and of the mortality of the body, which may be killed: whence we learn that the resurrection of the dead is a resurrection of the flesh; for unless it were raised again, it would be impossible for the flesh to be "killed in hell." But as a question may be here captiously raised about the meaning of "the body" (or "the flesh"), I will at once state that I understand by the human body nothing else than that fabric of the flesh which, whatever be the kind of material of which it is constructed and modified, is seen and handled, and sometimes indeed killed, by men. In like manner, I should not admit that anything but cement and stones and bricks form the body of a wall. If anyone imports into our argument some body of a subtle, secret nature, he must show, disclose, and prove to me that that identical body is the very one which was slain by human violence, and then (I will grant) that it is of such a body that (our scripture) speaks. If, again, the body or corporeal nature of the soul is cast in my teeth, it will only be an idle subterfuge! For since both substances are set before us (in this passage, which affirms) that "body and soul" are destroyed in hell, a distinction is obviously made between the two; and we are left to understand the body to be that which is tangible to us, that is, the flesh, which, as it will be destroyed in hell— since it did not "rather fear" being destroyed by God—so also will it be restored to life eternal, since it preferred to be killed by human hands. If, therefore, any one shall violently suppose that the destruction of the soul and the flesh in hell amounts to a final annihilation of the two substances, and not to their penal treatment (as if they were to be consumed, not punished), let him recollect that the fire of hell is eternal—expressly announced as an everlasting penalty; and let him then admit that it is from this circumstance that this never-ending "killing" is more formidable than a merely human murder, which is only temporal. He will then come to the conclusion that substances must be eternal, when their penal "killing" is an eternal one. Since, then, the body after the resurrection has to be killed by God in hell along with the soul, we surely have sufficient information in this fact respecting both the issues which await it, namely the resurrection of the flesh, and its eternal "killing." Else it would be most absurd if the flesh should be raised up and destined to "the killing in hell," in order to be put an end to, when it might suffer such an annihilation (more directly) if not raised again at all. A pretty paradox, to be sure, that an essence must be refitted with life, in order that it may receive that annihilation which has already in fact accrued to it! But Christ, whilst confirming us in the selfsame hope, adds the example of "the sparrows"—how that "not one of them falls to the ground without the will of God." He says this, that you may believe that the flesh which has been consigned to the ground, is able in like manner to rise again by the will of the same God. For although this is not allowed to the sparrows, yet "we are of more value than many sparrows," for the very reason that, when fallen, we rise again. He affirms, lastly, that "the very hairs of our head are all numbered," and in the affirmation He of course includes the promise of their safety; for if they were to be lost, where would be the use of having taken such a numerical care of them? Surely the only use lies (in this truth): "That of all which the Father hath given to me, I should lose none,"—not even a hair, as also not an eye nor a tooth. And yet whence shall come that "weeping and gnashing of teeth," if not from eyes and teeth?—even at that time when the body shall be slain in hell, and thrust out into that outer darkness which shall be the suitable torment of the eyes. He also who shall not be clothed at the marriage feast in the raiment of good works, will have to be "bound hand and foot,"—as being, of course, raised in his body. So, again, the very reclining at the feast in the kingdom of God, and sitting on Christ's thrones, and standing at last on His right hand and His left, and eating of the tree of life: what are all these but most certain proofs of a bodily appointment and destination?

Chapter XXXVI—Christ's Refutation of the Sadducees, and Affirmation of Catholic Doctrine.

Let us now see whether (the Lord) has not imparted greater strength to our doctrine in breaking down the subtle cavil of the Sadducees. Their great object, I take it, was to do away altogether with the resurrection, for the Sadducees in fact did not admit any salvation either for the soul or the flesh; and therefore, taking the strongest case they could for impairing the credibility of the resurrection, they adapted an argument from it in support of the question which they started. Their specious inquiry concerned the flesh, whether or not it would be subject to marriage after the resurrection; and they assumed the case of a woman who had married seven brothers, so that it was a doubtful point to which of them she should be restored. Now, let the purport both of the question and the answer be kept steadily in view, and the discussion is settled at once. For since the Sadducees indeed denied the resurrection, whilst the Lord affirmed it; since, too, (in affirming it,) He reproached them as being both ignorant of the Scriptures—those, of course which had declared the resurrection—as well as incredulous of the power of God, though, of course, effectual to raise the dead, and lastly, since He immediately added the words, "Now, that the dead are raised," (speaking) without misgiving, and affirming the very thing which was being denied, even the resurrection of the dead before Him who is "the God of the living,"—(it clearly follows) that He affirmed this verity in the precise sense in which they were denying it; that it was, in fact, the resurrection of the two natures of man. Nor does it follow, (as they would have it,) that because Christ denied that men would marry, He therefore proved that they would not rise again. On the contrary, He called them "the children of the resurrection," in a certain sense having by the resurrection to undergo a birth; and after that they marry no more, but in their risen life are "equal unto the angels," inasmuch as they are not to marry, because they are not to die, but are destined to pass into the angelic state by putting on the raiment of incorruption, although with a change in the substance which is restored to life. Besides, no question could be raised whether we are to marry or die again or not, without involving in doubt the restoration most especially of that substance which has a particular relation both to death and marriage—that is, the flesh. Thus, then, you have the Lord affirming against the Jewish heretics what is now encountering the denial of the Christian Sadducees—the resurrection of the entire man.

Chapter XXXVII.—Christ's Assertion About the Unprofitableness of the Flesh Explained Consistently with Our Doctrine.

He says, it is true, that "the flesh profiteth nothing;" but then, as in the former case, the meaning must be regulated by the subject which is spoken of. Now, because they thought His discourse was harsh and intolerable, supposing that He had really and literally enjoined on them to eat his flesh, He, with the view of ordering the state of salvation as a spiritual thing, set out with the principle, "It is the spirit that quickeneth;" and then added, "The flesh profiteth nothing,"—meaning, of course, to the giving of life. He also goes on to explain what He would have us to understand by spirit: "The words that I speak unto you, they are spirit, and they are life." In a like sense He had previously said: "He that heareth my words, and believeth on Him that sent me, hath everlasting life, and shall not come into condemnation, but shall pass from death unto life." Constituting, therefore, His word as the life-giving principle, because that word is spirit and life, He likewise called His flesh by the same appellation; because, too, the Word had become flesh, we ought therefore to desire Him in order that we may have life, and to devour Him with the ear, and to ruminate on Him with the understanding, and to digest Him by faith. Now, just before (the passage in hand), He had declared His flesh to be "the bread which cometh down from heaven," impressing on (His hearers) constantly under the figure of necessary food the memory of their forefathers, who had preferred the bread and flesh of Egypt to their divine calling. Then, turning His subject to their reflections, because He perceived that they were going to be scattered from Him, He says: "The flesh profiteth nothing." Now what is there to destroy the resurrection of the flesh? As if there might not reasonably enough be something which, although it "profiteth nothing" itself, might yet be capable of being profited by something else. The spirit "profiteth," for it imparts life. The flesh profiteth nothing, for it is subject to death. Therefore, He has rather put the two propositions in a way which favors our belief: for by showing what "profits," and what "does not profit," He has likewise thrown light on the object which receives as well as the subject which gives the "profit." Thus, in the present instance, we have the Spirit giving life to the flesh which has been subdued by death; for "the hour," says He, "is coming, when the dead shall hear the voice of the Son of God, and they that hear shall live." Now, what is "the dead" but the flesh? and what is "the voice of God" but the Word? and what is the Word but the Spirit, who shall justly raise the flesh which He had once Himself become, and that too from death, which He Himself suffered, and from the grave, which He Himself once entered? Then again, when He says, "Marvel not at this: for the hour is coming, in which all that are in the graves shall hear the voice of the Son of God, and shall come forth; they that have done good, to the resurrection of life; and they that have done evil, unto the resurrection of damnation,"—none will after such words be able to interpret the dead "that are in the graves" as any other than the bodies of the flesh, because the graves themselves are nothing but the resting-place of corpses: for it is incontestable that even those who partake of "the old man," that is to say, sinful men—in other words, those who are dead through their ignorance of God (whom our heretics, forsooth, foolishly insist on understanding by the word "graves")—are plainly here spoken of as having to come from their graves for judgment. But how are graves to come forth from graves?

Chapter XXXVIII—Christ, by Raising the Dead, Attested in a Practical Way the Doctrine of the Resurrection of the Flesh.

After the Lord's words, what are we to think of the purport of His actions, when He raises dead persons from their biers and their graves? To what end did He do so? If it was only for the mere exhibition of His power, or to afford the temporary favor of restoration to life, it was really no great matter for Him to raise men to die over again. If, however, as was the truth, it was rather to put in secure keeping men's belief in a future resurrection, then it must follow from the particular form of His own examples, that the said resurrection will be a bodily one. I can never allow it to be said that the resurrection of the future, being destined for the soul only, did then receive these preliminary illustrations of a raising of the flesh, simply because it would have been impossible to have shown the resurrection of an invisible soul except by the resuscitation of a visible substance. They have but a poor knowledge of God, who suppose Him to be only capable of doing what comes within the compass of their own thoughts; and after all, they cannot but know full well what His capability has ever been, if they only make acquaintance with the writings of John. For unquestionably he, who has exhibited to our sight the martyrs' hitherto disembodied souls resting under the altar, was quite able to display them before our eyes rising without a body of flesh. I, however, for my part prefer (believing) that it is impossible for God to practice deception (weak as He only could be in respect of artifice), from any fear of seeming to have given preliminary proofs of a thing in a way which is inconsistent with His actual disposal of the thing; nay more, from a fear that, since He was not powerful enough to show us a sample of the resurrection without the flesh, He might with still greater infirmity be unable to display (by and by) the full accomplishment of the sample in the self-same substance of the flesh. No example, indeed, is greater than the thing of which it is a sample. Greater, however, it is, if souls with their body are to be raised as the evidence of their resurrection without the body, so as that the entire salvation of man in soul and body should become a guarantee for only the half, the soul; whereas the condition in all examples is, that which would be deemed the less—I mean the resurrection of the soul only—should be the foretaste, as it were, of the rising of the flesh also at its appointed time. And therefore, according to our estimate of the truth, those examples of dead persons who were raised by the Lord were indeed a proof of the resurrection both of the flesh and of the soul—a proof, in fact, that this gift was to be denied to neither substance. Considered, however, as examples only, they expressed all the less significance—less, indeed, than Christ will express at last—for they were not raised up for glory and immortality, but only for another death.

Chapter XXXIX. —Additional Evidence Afforded to Us in the Acts of the Apostles.

The Acts of the Apostles, too, attest the resurrection. Now the apostles had nothing else to do, at least among the Jews, than to explain the Old Testament and confirm the New, and above all, to preach God in Christ. Consequently, they introduced nothing new concerning the resurrection, besides announcing it to the glory of Christ: in every other respect it had been already received in simple and intelligent faith, without any question as to what sort of resurrection it was to be, and without encountering any other opponents than the Sadducees. So much easier was it to deny the resurrection altogether, than to understand it in an alien sense. You find Paul confessing his faith before the chief priests, under the shelter of the chief captain, among the Sadducees and the Pharisees: "Men and brethren," he says, "I am a Pharisee, the son of a Pharisee; of the hope and resurrection of the dead I am now called in question by you," —referring, of course, to the nation's hope; in order to avoid, in his present condition, as an apparent transgressor of the law, being thought to approach to the Sadducees in opinion on the most important article of the faith—even the resurrection. That belief, therefore, in the resurrection which he would not appear to impair, he really confirmed in the opinion of the Pharisees, since he rejected the views of the Sadducees, who denied it. In like manner, before Agrippa also, he says that he was advancing "none other things than those which the prophets had announced." He was therefore maintaining just such a resurrection as the prophets had foretold. He mentions also what is written by "Moses," touching the resurrection of the dead; (and in so doing) he must have known that it would be a rising in the body, since requisition will have to be made therein of the blood of man. He declared it then to be of such a character as the Pharisees had admitted it, and such as the Lord had Himself maintained it, and such too as the Sadducees refused to believe it—such refusal leading them indeed to an absolute rejection of the whole verity. Nor had the Athenians previously understood Paul to announce any other resurrection. They had, in fact, derided his announcement; but they would have indulged no such derision if they had heard from him nothing but the restoration of the soul, for they would have received that as the very common anticipation of their own native philosophy. But when the preaching of the resurrection, of which they had previously not heard, by its absolute novelty excited the heathen, and a not unnatural incredulity in so wonderful a matter began to harass the simple faith with many discussions, then the apostle took care in almost every one of his writings to strengthen men's belief of this Christian hope, pointing out that there was such a hope, and that it had not as yet been realized, and that it would be in the body,—a point which was the especial object of inquiry, and, what was besides a doubtful question, not in a body of a different kind from ours.

Chapter XL—Sundry Passages of St. Paul Which Attest Our Doctrine Rescued from the Perversions of Heresy.

Now it is no matter of surprise if arguments are captiously taken from the writings of (the apostle) himself, inasmuch as there "must needs be heresies;" but these could not be, if the Scriptures were not capable of a false interpretation. Well, then, heresies finding that the apostle had mentioned two "men"—"the inner man," that is, the soul, and "the outward man," that is, the flesh—awarded salvation to the soul or inward man, and destruction to the flesh or outward man, because it is written (in the Epistle) to the Corinthians: "Though our outward man decayeth, yet the inward man is renewed day by day." Now, neither the soul by itself alone is "man" (it was subsequently implanted in the clayey mold to which the name man had been already given), nor is the flesh without the soul "man": for after the exile of the soul from it, it has the title of corpse. Thus the designation man is, in a certain sense, the bond between the two closely united substances, under which designation they cannot but be coherent natures. As for the inward man, indeed, the apostle prefers its being regarded as the mind and heart rather than the soul; in other words, not so much the substance itself as the savor of the substance. Thus when, writing to the Ephesians, he spoke of "Christ dwelling in their inner man," he meant, no doubt, that the Lord ought to be admitted into their senses. He then added, "in your hearts by faith, rooted and grounded in love,"— making "faith" and "love" not substantial parts, but only conceptions of the soul. But when he used the phrase "in your hearts," seeing that these are substantial parts of the flesh, he at once assigned to the flesh the actual "inward man," which he placed in the heart. Consider now in what sense he alleged that "the outward man decayeth, while the inward man is renewed day by day." You certainly would not maintain that he could mean that corruption of the flesh which it undergoes from the moment of death, in its appointed state of perpetual decay; but the wear and tear which for the name of Christ it experiences during its course of life before and until death, in harassing cares and tribulations as well as in tortures and persecutions. Now the inward man will have, of course, to be renewed by the suggestion of the Spirit, advancing by faith and holiness day after day, herein this life, not thereafter the resurrection, were our renewal is not a gradual process from day to day, but a consummation once for all complete. You may learn this, too, from the following passage, where the apostle says: "For our light affliction, which is but for a moment, worketh for us a far more exceeding and eternal weight of glory; while we look not at the things which are seen," that is, our sufferings, "but at the things which are not seen," that is, our rewards: "for the things which are seen are temporal, but the things which are not seen are eternal." For the afflictions and injuries wherewith the outward man is worn away, he affirms to be only worthy of being despised by us, as being light and temporary; preferring those eternal recompenses which are also invisible, and that "weight of glory" which will be a counterpoise for the labors in the endurance of which the flesh here suffers decay. So that the subject in this passage is not that corruption which they ascribe to the outward man in the utter destruction of the flesh, with the view of nullifying the resurrection. So also he says elsewhere: "If so be that we suffer with Him, that we may be also glorified together; for I reckon that the sufferings of the present time are not worthy to be compared with the glory that shall be revealed in us." Here again he shows us that our sufferings are less than their rewards. Now, since it is through the flesh that we suffer with Christ—for it is the property of the flesh to be worn by sufferings—to the same flesh belongs the recompense which is promised for suffering with Christ. Accordingly, when he is going to assign afflictions to the flesh as its especial liability—according to the statement he had already made—he says, "When we were come into Macedonia, our flesh had no rest;" then, in order to make the soul a fellow-sufferer with the body, he adds, "We were troubled on every side; without were fightings," which of course warred down the flesh, "within were fears," which afflicted the soul. Although, therefore, the outward man decays—not in the sense of missing the resurrection, but of enduring tribulation—it will be understood from this scripture that it is not exposed to its suffering without the inward man. Both therefore, will be glorified together, even as they have suffered together. Parallel with their participation in troubles, must necessarily run their association also in rewards.

Chapter XLI—The Dissolution of Our Tabernacle Consistent with the Resurrection of Our Bodies.

It is still the same sentiment which he follows up in the passage in which he puts the recompense above the sufferings: "for we know;" he says, "that if our earthly house of this tabernacle were dissolved, we have a house not made with hands, eternal in the heavens;" in other words, owing to the fact that our flesh is undergoing dissolution through its sufferings, we shall be provided with a home in heaven. He remembered the award (which the Lord assigns) in the Gospel: "Blessed are they who are persecuted for righteousness' sake, for theirs is the kingdom of heaven." Yet, when he thus contrasted the recompense of the reward, he did not deny the flesh's restoration; since the recompense is due to the same substance to which the dissolution is attributed—that is, of course, the flesh. Because, however, he had called the flesh a house, he wished elegantly to use the same term in his comparison of the ultimate reward; promising to the very house, which undergoes dissolution through suffering, a better house through the resurrection. Just as the Lord also promises us many mansions as of a house in His Father's home; although this may possibly be understood of the domicile of this world, on the dissolution of whose fabric an eternal abode is promised in heaven, inasmuch as the following context, having a manifest reference to the flesh, seems to show that these preceding words have no such reference. For the apostle makes a distinction, when he goes on to say, "For in this we groan, earnestly desiring to be clothed upon with our house which is from heaven, if so be that being clothed we shall not be found naked;" which means, before we put off the garment of the flesh, we wish to be clothed with the celestial glory of immortality. Now the privilege of this favor awaits those who shall at the coming of the Lord be found in the flesh, and who shall, owing to the oppressions of the time of Antichrist, deserve by an instantaneous death, which is accomplished by a sudden change, to become qualified to join the rising saints; as he writes to the Thessalonians: "For this we say unto you by the word of the Lord, that we which are alive and remain unto the coming of the Lord shall not prevent them which are asleep. For the Lord Himself shall descend from heaven with a shout, with the voice of the archangel, and with the trump of God: and the dead in Christ shall rise first: then we too shall ourselves be caught up together with them in the clouds, to meet the Lord in the air: and so shall we ever be with the Lord."

Chapter XLII. —Death Changes, Without Destroying, Our Mortal Bodies. Remains of the Giants.

It is the transformation these shall undergo which he explains to the Corinthians, when he writes: "We shall all indeed rise again (though we shall not all undergo the transformation) in a moment, in the twinkling of an eye, at the last trump"—for none shall experience this change but those only who shall be found in the flesh. "And the dead," he says, "shall be raised, and we shall be changed." Now, after a careful consideration of this appointed order, you will be able to adjust what follows to the preceding sense. For when he adds, "This corruptible must put on incorruption, and this mortal must put on immortality," this will assuredly be that house from heaven, with which we so earnestly desire to be clothed upon, whilst groaning in this our present body,—meaning, of course, over this flesh in which we shall be surprised at last; because he says that we are burdened whilst in this tabernacle, which we do not wish indeed to be stripped of, but rather to be in it clothed over, in such a way that mortality may be swallowed up of life, that is, by putting on over us whilst we are transformed that vesture which is from heaven. For who is there that will not desire, while he is in the flesh, to put on immortality, and to continue his life by a happy escape from death, through the transformation which must be experienced instead of it, without encountering too that Hades which will exact the very last farthing? Notwithstanding, he who has already traversed Hades is destined also to obtain the change after the resurrection. For from this circumstance it is that we definitively declare that the flesh will by all means rise again, and, from the change that is to come over it, will assume the condition of angels. Now, if it were merely in the case of those who shall be found in the flesh that the change must be undergone, in order that mortality may be swallowed up of life—in other words, that the flesh (be covered) with the heavenly and eternal raiment—it would either follow that those who shall be found in death would not obtain life, deprived as they would then be of the material and so to say the aliment of life, that is, the flesh; or else, these also must needs undergo the change, that in them too mortality may be swallowed up of life, since it is appointed that they too should obtain life. But, you say, in the case of the dead, mortality is already swallowed up of life. No, not in all cases, certainly. For how many will most probably be found of men who had just died—so recently put into their graves, that nothing in them would seem to be decayed? For you do not of course deem a thing to be decayed unless it be cut off, abolished, and withdrawn from our perception, as having in every possible way ceased to be apparent. There are the carcasses of the giants of old time; it will be obvious enough that they are not absolutely decayed, for their bony frames are still extant. We have already spoken of this elsewhere. For instance, even lately in this very city, when they were sacrilegiously laying the foundations of the Odeum on a good many ancient graves, people were horror-stricken to discover, after some five hundred years, bones, which still retained their moisture, and hair which had not lost its perfume. It is certain not only that bones remain indurated, but also that teeth continue undecayed for ages—both of them the lasting germs of that body which is to sprout into life again in the resurrection. Lastly, even if everything that is mortal in all the dead shall then be found decayed—at any rate consumed by death, by time, and through age—is there nothing which will be "swallowed up of life," nor by being covered over and arrayed in the vesture of immortality? Now, he who says that mortality is going to be swallowed up of life has already admitted that what is dead is not destroyed by those other before-mentioned devourers. And verily it will be extremely fit that all shall be consummated and brought about by the operations of God, and not by the laws of nature. Therefore, inasmuch as what is mortal has to be swallowed up of life, it must needs be brought out to view in order to be so swallowed up; (needful) also to be swallowed up, in order to undergo the ultimate transformation. If you were to say that a fire is to be lighted, you could not possibly allege that what is to kindle it is sometimes necessary and sometimes not. In like manner, when he inserts the words "If so be that being unclothed we be not found naked,"—referring, of course, to those who shall not be found in the day of the Lord alive and in the flesh—he did not say that they whom he had just described as unclothed or stripped, were naked in any other sense than meaning that they should be understood to be reinvested with the very same substance they had been divested of. For although they shall be found naked when their flesh has been laid aside, or to some extent sundered or worn away (and this condition may well be called nakedness,) they shall afterwards recover it again, in order that, being reinvested with the flesh, they may be able also to have put over that the supervestment of immortality; for it will be impossible for the outside garment to fit except over one who is already dressed.

Chapter XLIII. —No Disparagement of Our Doctrine in St. Paul's Phrase, Which Calls Our Residence in the Flesh Absence from the Lord.

In the same way, when he says, "Therefore we are always confident, and fully aware, that while we are at home in the body we are absent from the Lord; for we walk by faith, not be sight," it is manifest that in this statement there is no design of disparaging the flesh, as if it separated us from the Lord. For there is here pointedly addressed to us an exhortation to disregard this present life, since we are absent from the Lord as long as we are passing through it—walking by faith, not by sight; in other words, in hope, not in reality. Accordingly, he adds: "We are indeed confident and deem it good rather to be absent from the body, and present with the Lord;" in order, that is, that we may walk by sight rather than by faith, in realization rather than in hope. Observe how he here also ascribes to the excellence of martyrdom a contempt for the body. For no one, on becoming absent from the body, is at once a dweller in the presence of the Lord, except by the prerogative of martyrdom, he gains a lodging in Paradise, not in the lower regions. Now, had the apostle been at a loss for words to describe the departure from the body? Or does he purposely use a novel phraseology? For, wanting to express our temporary absence from the body, he says that we are strangers, absent from it, because a man who goes abroad returns after a while to his home. Then he says even to all: "We therefore earnestly desire to be acceptable unto God, whether absent or present; for we must all appear before the judgment-seat of Christ Jesus." If all of us, then all of us wholly; if wholly, then our inward man and outward too—that is, our bodies no less than our souls. "That everyone," as he goes on to say, "may receive the things done in his body, according to that he hath done, whether it be good or bad." Now I ask, how do you read this passage? Do you take it to be confusedly constructed, with a transposition of ideas? Is the question about what things will have to be received by the body, or the things which have been already done in the body? Well, if the things which are to be borne by the body are meant, then undoubtedly a resurrection of the body is implied; and if the things which have been already done in the body are referred to, (the same conclusion follows): for of course the retribution will have to be paid by the body, since it was by the body that the actions were performed. Thus the apostle's whole argument from the beginning is unraveled in this concluding clause, wherein the resurrection of the flesh is set forth; and it ought to be understood in a sense which is strictly in accordance with this conclusion.

Chapter XLIV—Sundry Other Passages of St. Paul Explained in a Sentence Confirmatory of Our Doctrine.

Now, if you will examine the words which precede the passage where mention is made of the outward and the inward man, will you not discover the whole truth, both of the dignity and the hope of the flesh? For, when he speaks of the "light which God hath commanded to shine in our hearts, to give the light of the knowledge of the glory of the Lord in the person of Jesus Christ," and says that "we have this treasure in earthen vessels," meaning of course the flesh, which is meant—that the flesh shall be destroyed, because it is "an earthen vessel," deriving its origin from clay; or that it is to be glorified, as being the receptacle of a divine treasure? Now if that true light, which is in the person of Christ, contains in itself life, and that life with its light is committed to the flesh, is that destined to perish which has life entrusted to it? Then, of course, the treasure will perish also; for perishable things are entrusted to things which are themselves perishable, which is like putting new wine into old bottles. When also he adds, "Always bearing about in our body the dying of the Lord Jesus Christ," what sort of substance is that which, after (being called) the temple of God, can now be also designated the tomb of Christ? But why do we bear about in the body the dying of the Lord? In order, as he says, "that His life also may be manifested." Where? "In the body." In what body? "In our mortal body." Therefore, in the flesh, which is mortal indeed through sin, but living through grace—how great a grace you may see when the purpose is, "that the life of Christ may be manifested in it." Is it then in a thing which is a stranger to salvation, in a substance which is perpetually dissolved, that the life of Christ will be manifested, which is eternal, continuous, incorruptible, and already the life of God? Else to what epoch belongs that life of the Lord which is to be manifested in our body? It surely is the life which He lived up to His passion, which was not only openly shown among the Jews, but has now been displayed even to all nations. Therefore, that life is meant which "has broken the adamantine gates of death and the brazen bars of the lower world,"—a life which thenceforth has been and will be ours. Lastly, it is to be manifested in the body. When? After death. How? By rising in our body, as Christ also rose in His. But lest anyone should here object, that the life of Jesus has even now to be manifested in our body by the discipline of holiness, and patience, and righteousness, and wisdom, in which the Lord's life abounded, the most provident wisdom of the apostle inserts this purpose: "For we which live are always delivered unto death for Jesus' sake, that His life may be manifested in our mortal body." In us, therefore, even when dead, does he say that this is to take place in us. And if so, how is this possible except in our body after its resurrection? Therefore, he adds in the concluding sentence: "Knowing that He which raised up the Lord Jesus, shall raise up us also with Him," risen as He is already from the dead. But perhaps "with Him" means "like Him:" well then, if it be like Him, it is not of course without the flesh.

Chapter XLV—The Old Man and the New Man of St. Paul Explained.

But in their blindness they again impale themselves on the point of the old and the new man. When the apostle enjoins us "to put off the old man, which is corrupt according to the deceitful lusts; and to be renewed in the spirit of our mind; and to put on the new man, which after God is created in righteousness and true holiness," (they maintain) that by here also making a distinction between the two substances, and applying the old one to the flesh and the new one to the spirit, he ascribes to the old man—that is to say, the flesh—a permanent corruption. Now, if you follow the order of the substances, the soul cannot be the new man because it comes the later of the two; nor can the flesh be the old man because it is the former. For what fraction of time was it that intervened between the creative hand of God and His afflatus? I will venture to say, that even if the soul was a good deal prior to the flesh, by the very circumstance that the soul had to wait to be itself completed, it made the other really the former. For everything which gives the finishing stroke and perfection to a work, although it is subsequent in its mere order, yet has the priority in its effect. Much more is that prior, without which preceding things could have no existence. If the flesh be the old man, when did it become so? From the beginning? But Adam was wholly a new man, and of that new man there could be no part an old man. And from that time, ever since the blessing which was pronounced upon man's generation, the flesh and the soul have had a simultaneous birth, without any calculable difference in time; so that the two have been even generated together in the womb, as we have shown in our Treatise on the Soul. Contemporaneous in the womb, they are also temporally identical in their birth. The two are no doubt produced by human parents of two substances, but not at two different periods; rather they are so entirely one, that neither is before the other in point of time. It is more correct (to say), that we are either entirely the old man or entirely the new, for we cannot tell how we can possibly be anything else. But the apostle mentions a very clear mark of the old man. For "put off," says he, "concerning the former conversation, the old man;" (he does) not say concerning the seniority of either substance. It is not indeed the flesh which he bids us to put off, but the works which he in another passage shows to be "works of the flesh." He brings no accusation against men's bodies, of which he even writes as follows: "Putting away lying, speak every man truth with his neighbor: for we are members one of another. Be ye angry, and sin not: let not the sun go down upon your wrath: neither give place to the devil. Let him that stole steal no more: but rather let him labor, working with his hands (the thing which is good), that he may have to give to him that needeth. Let no corrupt communication proceed out of your mouth, but that which is good for the edification of faith, that it may minister grace unto the hearers. And grieve not the Holy Spirit of God, whereby ye are sealed unto the day of redemption. Let all bitterness, and wrath, and anger, and clamor, and evil-speaking, be put away from you, with all malice: but be ye kind one to another, tender-hearted, forgiving one another, even as God in Christ hath forgiven you." Why, therefore, do not those who suppose the flesh to be the old man, hasten their own death, in order that by laying aside the old man they may satisfy the apostle's precepts? As for ourselves, we believe that the whole of faith is to be administered in the flesh, nay more, by the flesh, which has both a mouth for the utterance of all holy words, and a tongue to refrain from blasphemy, and a heart to avoid all irritation, and hands to labor and to give; while we also maintain that as well the old man as the new has relation to the difference of moral conduct, and not to any discrepancy of nature. And just as we acknowledge that that which according to its former conversation was "the old man" was also corrupt, and received its very name in accordance with "its deceitful lusts," so also (do we hold) that it is "the old man in reference to its former conversation," and not in respect of the flesh through any permanent dissolution. Moreover, it is still unimpaired in the flesh, and identical in that nature, even when it has become "the new man;" since it is of its sinful course of life, and not of its corporeal substance, that it has been divested.

Chapter XLVI. —It is the Works of the Flesh, Not the Substance of the Flesh, Which St. Paul Always Condemns.

You may notice that the apostle everywhere condemns the works of the flesh in such a way as to appear to condemn the flesh; but no one can suppose him to have any such view as this, since he goes on to suggest another sense, even though somewhat resembling it. For when he actually declares that "they who are in the flesh cannot please God," he immediately recalls the statement from a heretical sense to a sound one, by adding, "But ye are not in the flesh, but in the Spirit." Now, by denying them to be in the flesh who yet obviously were in the flesh, he showed that they were not living amidst the works of the flesh, and therefore that they who could not please God were not those who were in the flesh, but only those who were living after the flesh; whereas they pleased God, who, although existing in the flesh, were yet walking after the Spirit. And, again, he says that "the body is dead;" but it is "because of sin," even as "the Spirit is life because of righteousness." When, however, he thus sets life in opposition to the death which is constituted in the flesh, he unquestionably promises the life of righteousness to the same state for which he determined the death of sin. But unmeaning is this opposition which he makes between the "life" and the "death," if the life is not there where that very thing is to which he opposes it—even the death which is to be extirpated of course from the body. Now, if life thus extirpates death from the body, it can accomplish this only by penetrating thither where that is which it is excluding. But why am I resorting to knotty arguments, when the apostle treats the subject with perfect plainness? "For if," says he, "the Spirit of Him that raised up Jesus from the dead dwell in you, He that raised up Jesus from the dead shall also quicken your mortal bodies, because of His Spirit that dwelleth in you;" so that even if a person were to assume that the soul is "the mortal body," he would (since he cannot possibly deny that the flesh is this also) be constrained to acknowledge a restoration even of the flesh, in consequence of its participation in the selfsame state. From the following words, moreover, you may learn that it is the works of the flesh which are condemned, and not the flesh itself: "Therefore, brethren, we are debtors, not to the flesh, to live after the flesh: for if ye live after the flesh ye shall die; but if ye, through the Spirit, do mortify the deeds of the body, ye shall live." Now (that I may answer each point separately), since salvation is promised to those who are living in the flesh, but walking after the Spirit, it is no longer the flesh which is an adversary to salvation, but the working of the flesh. When, however, this operativeness of the flesh is done away with, which is the cause of death, the flesh is shown to be safe, since it is freed from the cause of death. "For the law," says he, "of the Spirit of life in Christ Jesus hath made me free from the law of sin and death,"—that, surely, which he previously mentioned as dwelling in our members. Our members, therefore, will no longer be subject to the law of death, because they cease to serve that of sin, from both which they have been set free. "For what the law could not do, in that it was weak through the flesh, God sending His own Son in the likeness of sinful flesh, and through sin condemned sin in the flesh,"—not the flesh in sin, for the house is not to be condemned with its inhabitant. He said, indeed, that "sin dwelleth in our body." But the condemnation of sin is the acquittal of the flesh, just as its non-condemnation subjugates it to the law of sin and death. In like manner, he called "the carnal mind" first "death," and afterwards "enmity against God;" but he never predicated this of the flesh itself. But to what then, you will say, must the carnal mind be ascribed, if it be not to the carnal substance itself? I will allow your objection, if you will prove to me that the flesh has any discernment of its own. If, however, it has no conception of anything without the soul, you must understand that the carnal mind must be referred to the soul, although ascribed sometimes to the flesh, on the ground that it is ministered to for the flesh and through the flesh. And therefore (the apostle) says that "sin dwelleth in the flesh," because the soul by which sin is provoked has its temporary lodging in the flesh, which is doomed indeed to death, not however on its own account, but on account of sin. For he says in another passage also: "How is it that you conduct yourselves as if you were even now living in the world?" where he is not writing to dead persons, but to those who ought to have ceased to live after the ways of the world.

Chapter XLVII. —St. Paul, All Through, Promises Eternal Life to the Body.

For that must be living after the world, which, as the old man, he declares to be "crucified with Christ," not as a bodily structure, but as moral behavior. Besides, if we do not understand it in this sense, it is not our bodily frame which has been transfixed (at all events), nor has our flesh endured the cross of Christ; but the sense is that which he has subjoined, "that the body of sin might be made void," by an amendment of life, not by a destruction of the substance, as he goes on to say, "that henceforth we should not serve sin;" and that we should believe ourselves to be "dead with Christ," in such a manner as that "we shall also live with Him." On the same principle he says: "Likewise reckon ye also yourselves to be dead indeed." To what? To the flesh? No, but "unto sin." Accordingly, as to the flesh they will be saved—"alive unto God in Christ Jesus," through the flesh of course, to which they will not be dead; since it is "unto sin," and not to the flesh, that they are dead. For he pursues the point still further: "Let not sin therefore reign in your mortal body, that ye should obey it, and that ye should yield your members as instruments of unrighteousness unto sin: but yield ye yourselves unto God, as those that are alive from the dead"—not simply alive, but as alive from the dead—"and your members as instruments of righteousness." And again: "As ye have yielded your members servants of uncleanness, and of iniquity unto iniquity, even so now yield your members servants of righteousness unto holiness; for whilst ye were the servants of sin, ye were free from righteousness. What fruit had ye then in those things of which ye are now ashamed? For the end of those things is death. But now, being made free from sin, and become servants to God, ye have your fruit unto holiness, and the end everlasting life. For the wages of sin is death, but the gift of God is eternal life through Jesus Christ our Lord." Thus throughout this series of passages, whilst withdrawing our members from unrighteousness and sin, and applying them to righteousness and holiness, and transferring the same from the wages of death to the donative of eternal life, he undoubtedly promises to the flesh the recompense of salvation. Now it would not at all have been consistent that any rule of holiness and righteousness should be especially enjoined for the flesh, if the reward of such a discipline were not also within its reach; nor could even baptism be properly ordered for the flesh, if by its regeneration a course were not inaugurated tending to its restitution; the apostle himself suggesting this idea: "Know ye not, that so many of us as are baptized into Jesus Christ, are baptized into His death? We are therefore buried with Him by baptism into death, that just as Christ was raised up from the dead, even so we also should walk in newness of life." And that you may not suppose that this is said merely of that life which we have to walk in the newness of, through baptism, by faith, the apostle with superlative forethought adds: "For if we have been planted together in the likeness of Christ's death, we shall be also in the likeness of His resurrection." By a figure we die in our baptism, but in a reality we rise again in the flesh, even as Christ did, "that, as sin has reigned in death, so also grace might reign through righteousness unto life eternal, through Jesus Christ our Lord." But how so, unless equally in the flesh? For where the death is, there too must be the life after the death, because also the life was first there, where the death subsequently was. Now, if the dominion of death operates only in the dissolution of the flesh, in like manner death's contrary, life, ought to produce the contrary effect, even the restoration of the flesh; so that, just as death had swallowed it up in its strength, it also, after this mortal was swallowed up of immortality, may hear the challenge pronounced against it: "O death, where is thy sting? O grave, where is thy victory?" For in this way "grace shall there much more abound, where sin once abounded." In this way also "shall strength be made perfect in weakness,"—saving what is lost, reviving what is dead, healing what is stricken, curing what is faint, redeeming what is lost, freeing what is enslaved, recalling what has strayed, raising what is fallen; and this from earth to heaven, where, as the apostle teaches the Philippians, "we have our citizenship, from whence also we look for our Savior Jesus Christ, who shall change our body of humiliation, that it may be fashioned like unto His glorious body"—of course after the resurrection, because Christ Himself was not glorified before

He suffered. These must be "the bodies" which he "beseeches" the Romans to "present" as "a living sacrifice, holy, acceptable unto God." But how a living sacrifice, if these bodies are to perish? How a holy one, if they are profanely soiled? How acceptable to God, if they are condemned? Come, now, tell me how that passage (in the Epistle) to the Thessalonians—which, because of its clearness, I should supposed to have been written with a sunbeam—is understood by our heretics, who shun the light of Scripture: "And the very God of peace sanctify you wholly." And as if this were not plain enough, it goes on to say: "And may your whole body, and soul, and spirit be preserved blameless unto the coming of the Lord." Here you have the entire substance of man destined to salvation, and that at no other time than at the coming of the Lord, which is the key of the resurrection.

Chapter XLVIII. —Sundry Passages in the Great Chapter of the Resurrection of the Dead Explained in Defense of Our Doctrine.

But "flesh and blood," you say, "cannot inherit the kingdom of God." We are quite aware that this too is written; but although our opponents place it in the front of the battle, we have intentionally reserved the objection until now, in order that we may in our last assault overthrow it, after we have removed out of the way all the questions which are auxiliary to it. However, they must contrive to recall to their mind even now our preceding arguments, in order that the occasion which originally suggested this passage may assist our judgment in arriving at its meaning. The apostle, as I take it, having set forth for the Corinthians the details of their church discipline, had summed up the substance of his own gospel, and of their belief in an exposition of the Lord's death and resurrection, for the purpose of deducing therefrom the rule of our hope, and the groundwork thereof. Accordingly, he subjoins this statement: "Now if Christ be preached that He rose from the dead, how say some among you that there is no resurrection of the dead? If there be no resurrection of the dead, then Christ is not risen: and if Christ be not risen, then is our preaching vain, and your faith is also vain. Yea, and we are found false witnesses of God; because we have testified of God that He raised up Christ, whom He raised not up, if so be that the dead rise not. For if the dead rise not, then is not Christ raised: and if Christ be not raised, your faith is vain, because ye are yet in your sins, and they which have fallen asleep in Christ are perished." Now, what is the point which he evidently labors hard to make us believe throughout this passage? The resurrection of the dead, you say, which was denied: he certainly wished it to be believed on the strength of the example which he adduced—the Lord's resurrection. Certainly, you say. Well now, is an example borrowed from different circumstances, or from like ones? From like ones, by all means, is your answer. How then did Christ rise again? In the flesh, or not? No doubt, since you are told that He "died according to the Scriptures," and "that He was buried according to the Scriptures," no otherwise than in the flesh, you will also allow that it was in the flesh that He was raised from the dead. For the very same body which fell in death, and which lay in the sepulcher, did also rise again; (and it was) not so much Christ in the flesh, as the flesh in Christ. If, therefore, we are to rise again after the example of Christ, who rose in the flesh, we shall certainly not rise according to that example, unless we also shall ourselves rise again in the flesh. "For," he says, "since by man came death, by man came also the resurrection of the dead." (This he says) in order, on the one hand, to distinguish the two authors—Adam of death, Christ of resurrection; and, on the other hand, to make the resurrection operate on the same substance as the death, by comparing the authors themselves under the designation man. For if "as in Adam all die, even so in Christ shall all be made alive," their vivification in Christ must be in the flesh, since it is in the flesh that arises their death in Adam. "But every man in his own order," because of course it will be also every man in his own body. For the order will be arranged severally, on account of the individual merits. Now, as the merits must be ascribed to the body, it must needs follow that the order also should be arranged in respect of the bodies, that it may be in relation to their merits. But inasmuch as "some are also baptized for the dead," we will see whether there be a good reason for this. Now it is certain that they adopted this (practice) with such a presumption as made them suppose that the vicarious baptism (in question) would be beneficial to the flesh of another in anticipation of the resurrection; for unless it were a bodily resurrection, there would be no pledge secured by this process of a corporeal baptism. "Why are they then baptized for the dead," he asks, unless the bodies rise again which are thus baptized? For it is not the soul which is sanctified by the baptismal bath: its sanctification comes from the "answer." "And why," he inquires, "stand we in jeopardy every hour?"—meaning, of course, through the flesh. "I die daily," (says he); that is, undoubtedly, in the perils of the body, in which "he even fought with beasts at Ephesus,"—even with those beasts which caused him such peril and trouble in Asia, to which he alludes in his second epistle to the same church of Corinth: "For we would not, brethren, have you ignorant of our trouble which came to us in Asia, that we were pressed above measure, above strength, insomuch that we despaired even of life." Now, if I mistake not, he enumerates all these particulars in order that in his unwillingness to have his conflicts in the flesh supposed to be useless, he may induce an unfaltering belief in the resurrection of the flesh. For useless must that conflict be deemed (which is sustained in a body) for which no resurrection is in prospect. "But some man will say, How are the dead to be raised? And with what body will they come?" Now here he discusses the qualities of bodies, whether it be the very same, or different ones, which men are to resume. Since, however, such a question as this must be regarded as a subsequent one, it will in passing be enough for us that the resurrection is determined to be a bodily one even from this, that it is about the quality of bodies that the inquiry arises.

Chapter XLIX. —The Same Subject Continued. What Does the Apostle Exclude from the Dead? Certainly Not the Substance of the Flesh.

We come now to the very gist of the whole question: What are the substances, and of what nature are they, which the apostle has disinherited of the kingdom of God? The preceding statements give us a clue to this point also. He says: "The first man is of the earth, earthy"—that is, made of dust, that is, Adam; "the second man is from heaven"—that is, the Word of God, which is Christ, in no other way, however, man (although "from heaven"), than as being Himself flesh and soul, just as a human being is, just as Adam was. Indeed, in a previous passage He is called "the second Adam," deriving the identity of His name from His participation in the substance, because not even Adam was flesh of human seed, in which Christ is also like Him. "As is the earthy, such are they also that are earthy; and as is the heavenly, such are they also that are heavenly." Such (does he mean), in substance; or first of all in training, and afterwards in the dignity and worth which that training aimed at acquiring? Not in substance, however, by any means will the earthy and the heavenly be separated, designated as they have been by the apostle once for all, as men. For even if Christ were the only true "heavenly," nay, super-celestial Being, He is still man, as composed of body and soul; and in no respect is He separated from the quality of "earthiness," owing to that condition of His which makes Him a partaker of both substances. In like manner, those also who after Him are heavenly, are understood to have this celestial quality predicated of them not from their present nature, but from their future glory; because in a preceding sentence, which originated this distinction respecting difference of dignity, there was shown to be "one glory in celestial bodies, and another in terrestrial ones,"—"one glory of the sun, and another glory of the moon, and another glory of the stars: for even one star differeth from another star in glory," although not in substance. Then, after having thus premised the difference in that worth or dignity which is even now to be aimed at, and then at last to be enjoyed, the apostle adds an exhortation, that we should both here in our training follow the example of Christ, and there attain His eminence in glory: "As we have borne the image of the earthy, let us also bear the image of the heavenly." We have indeed borne the image of the earthy, by our sharing in his transgression, by our participation in his death, by our banishment from Paradise. Now, although the image of Adam is here borne by is in the flesh, yet we are not exhorted to put off the flesh; but if not the flesh, it is the conversation, in order that we may then bear the image of the heavenly in ourselves,—no longer indeed the image of God, and no longer the image of a Being whose state is in heaven; but after the lineaments of Christ, by our walking here in holiness, righteousness, and truth. And so wholly intent on the inculcation of moral conduct is he throughout this passage, that he tells us we ought to bear the image of Christ in this flesh of ours, and in this period of instruction and discipline. For when he says "let us bear" in the imperative mood, he suits his words to the present life, in which man exists in no other substance than as flesh and soul; or if it is another, even the heavenly, substance to which this faith (of ours) looks forward, yet the promise is made to that substance to which the injunction is given to labor earnestly to merit its reward. Since, therefore, he makes the image both of the earthy and the heavenly consist of moral conduct—the one to be abjured, and the other to be pursued—and then consistently adds, "For this I say" (on account, that is, of what I have already said, because the conjunction "for" connects what follows with the preceding words) "that flesh and blood cannot inherit the kingdom of God,"—he means the flesh and blood to be understood in no other sense than the before-mentioned "image of the earthy;" and since this is reckoned to consist in "the old conversation," which old conversation receives not the kingdom of God, therefore flesh and blood, by not receiving the kingdom of God, are reduced to the life of the old conversation. Of course, as the apostle has never put the substance for the works of man, he cannot use such a construction here. Since, however he has declared of men which are yet alive in the flesh, that they "are not in the flesh," meaning that they are not living in the works of the flesh, you ought not to subvert its form nor its substance, but only the works done in the substance (of the flesh), alienating us from the kingdom of God. It is after displaying to the Galatians these pernicious works that he professes to warn them beforehand, even as he had "told them in time past, that they which do such things should not inherit the kingdom of God," even because they bore not the image of the heavenly, as they had borne the image of the earthy; and so, in consequence of their old conversation, they were to be regarded as nothing else than flesh and blood. But even if the apostle had abruptly thrown out the sentence that flesh and blood must be excluded from the kingdom of God, without any previous intimation of his meaning, would it not have been equally our duty to interpret these two substances as the old man abandoned to mere flesh and blood—in other words, to eating and drinking, one feature of which would be to speak against the faith of the resurrection: "Let us eat and drink, for to-morrow we die." Now, when the apostle parenthetically inserted this, he censured flesh and blood because of their enjoyment in eating and drinking.

Chapter L.—In What Sense Flesh and Blood are Excluded from the Kingdom of God.

Putting aside, however, all interpretations of this sort, which criminate the works of the flesh and blood, it may be permitted me to claim for the resurrection these very substances, understood in none other than their natural sense. For it is not the resurrection that is directly denied to flesh and blood, but the kingdom of God, which is incidental to the resurrection (for there is a resurrection of judgment also); and there is even a confirmation of the general resurrection of the flesh, whenever a special one is excepted. Now, when it is clearly stated what the condition is to which the resurrection does not lead, it is understood what that is to which it does lead; and, therefore, whilst it is in consideration of men's merits that a difference is made in their resurrection by their conduct in the flesh, and not by the substance thereof, it is evident even from this, that flesh and blood are excluded from the kingdom of God in respect of their sin, not of their substance; and although in respect of their natural condition they will rise again for the judgment, because they rise not for the kingdom. Again, I will say, "Flesh and blood cannot inherit the kingdom of God;" and justly (does the apostle declare this of them, considered) alone and in themselves, in order to show that the Spirit is still needed (to qualify them) for the kingdom. For it is "the Spirit that quickeneth" us for the kingdom of God; "the flesh profiteth nothing." There is, however, something else which can be profitable thereunto, that is, the Spirit; and through the Spirit, the works also of the Spirit. Flesh and blood, therefore, must in every case rise again, equally, in their proper quality. But they to whom it is granted to enter the kingdom of God, will have to put on the power of an incorruptible and immortal life; for without this, or before they are able to obtain it, they cannot enter into the kingdom of God. With good reason, then, flesh and blood, as we have already said, by themselves fail to obtain the kingdom of God. But inasmuch as "this corruptible (that is, the flesh) must put on incorruption, and this mortal (that is, the blood) must put on immortality," by the change which is to follow the resurrection, it will, for the best of reasons, happen that flesh and blood, after that change and investiture, will become able to inherit the kingdom of God—but not without the resurrection. Some will have it, that by the phrase "flesh and blood," because of its rite of circumcision, Judaism is meant, which is itself too alienated from the kingdom of God, as being accounted "the old or former conversation," and as being designated by this title in another passage of the apostle also, who, "when it pleased God to reveal to him His Son, to preach Him amongst the heathen, immediately conferred not with flesh and blood," as he writes to the Galatians, (meaning by the phrase) the circumcision, that is to say, Judaism.

Chapter LI.—The Session of Jesus in His Incarnate Nature at the Right Hand of God a Guarantee of the Resurrection of Our Flesh.

That, however, which we have reserved for a concluding argument, will now stand as a plea for all, and for the apostle himself, who in very deed would have to be charged with extreme indiscretion, if he had so abruptly, as some will have it, and as they say, blindfold, and so indiscriminately, and so unconditionally, excluded from the kingdom of God, and indeed from the court of heaven itself, all flesh and blood whatsoever; since Jesus is still sitting there at the right hand of the Father, man, yet God—the last Adam, yet the primary Word—flesh and blood, yet purer than ours—who "shall descend in like manner as He ascended into heaven" the same both in substance and form, as the angels affirmed, so as even to be recognized by those who pierced Him. Designated, as He is, "the Mediator between God and man," He keeps in His own self the deposit of the flesh which has been committed to Him by both parties—the pledge and security of its entire perfection. For as "He has given to us the earnest of the Spirit," so has He received from us the earnest of the flesh, and has carried it with Him into heaven as a pledge of that complete entirety which is one day to be restored to it. Be not disquieted, O flesh and blood, with any care; in Christ you have acquired both heaven and the kingdom of God. Otherwise, if they say that you are not in Christ, let them also say that Christ is not in heaven, since they have denied you heaven. Likewise, "neither shall corruption," says he, "inherit incorruption." This he says, not that you may take flesh and blood to be corruption, for they are themselves rather the subjects of corruption—I mean through death, since death does not so much corrupt, as actually consume, our flesh and blood. But inasmuch as he had plainly said that the works of the flesh and blood could not obtain the kingdom of God, with the view of stating this with accumulated stress, he deprived corruption itself—that is, death, which profits so largely by the works of the flesh and blood—from all inheritance of incorruption. For a little afterwards, he has described what is, as it were, the death of death itself: "Death," says he, "is swallowed up in victory. O death, where is thy sting? O grave, where is thy victory? The sting of death is sin"—here is the corruption; "and the strength of sin is the law"—that other law, no doubt, which he has described "in his members as warring against the law of his mind,"—meaning, of course, the actual power of sinning against his will. Now he says in a previous passage (of our Epistle to the Corinthians), that "the last enemy to be destroyed is death." In this way, then, it is that corruption shall not inherit incorruption; in other words, death shall not continue. When and how shall it cease? In that "moment, that twinkling of an eye, at the last trump, when the dead shall rise incorruptible." But what are these, if not they who were corruptible before— that is, our bodies; in other words, our flesh and blood? And we undergo the change. But in what condition, if not in that wherein we shall be found? "For this corruptible must put on incorruption, and this mortal must put on immortality." What mortal is this but the flesh? what corruptible but the blood. Moreover, that you may not suppose the apostle to have any other meaning, in his care to teach you, and that you may understand him seriously to apply his statement to the flesh, when he says "this corruptible" and "this mortal," he utters the words while touching the surface of his own body. He certainly could not have pronounced these phrases except in reference to an object which was palpable and apparent. The expression indicates a bodily exhibition. Moreover, a corruptible body is one thing, and corruption is another; so a mortal body is one thing, and mortality is another. For that which suffers is one thing, and that which causes it to suffer is another. Consequently, those things which are subject to corruption and mortality, even the flesh and blood, must needs also be susceptible of incorruption and immortality.

Chapter LII—From St. Paul's Analogy of the Seed We Learn that the Body Which Died Will Rise Again, Garnished with the Appliances of Eternal Life.

Let us now see in what body he asserts that the dead will come. And with a felicitous sally he proceeds at once to illustrate the point, as if an objector had plied him with some such question. "Thou fool," says he, "that which thou sowest is not quickened, except it die." From this example of the seed it is then evident that no other flesh is quickened than that which shall have undergone death, and therefore all the rest of the question will become clear enough. For nothing which is incompatible with the idea suggested by the example can possibly be understood; nor from the clause which follows, "That which thou sowest, thou sowest not the body which shall be," are you permitted to suppose that in the resurrection a different body is to arise from that which is sown in death. Otherwise you have run away from the example. For if wheat be sown and dissolved in the ground, barley does not spring up. Still it is not the very same grain in kind; nor is its nature the same, or its quality and form. Then whence comes it, if it is not the very same? For even the decay is a proof of the thing itself, since it is the decay of the actual grain. Well, but does not the apostle himself suggest in what sense it is that "the body which shall be" is not the body which is sown, even when he says, "But bare grain, it may chance of wheat, or of some other grain; but God giveth it a body as it pleaseth Him?" Gives it of course to the grain which he says is sown bare. No doubt, you say. Then the grain is safe enough, to which God has to assign a body. But how safe, if it is nowhere in existence, if it does not rise again if it rises not again its actual self? If it rises not again, it is not safe; and if it is not even safe, it cannot receive a body from God. But there is every possible proof that it is safe. For what purpose, therefore, will God give it "a body, as it pleases Him," even when it already has its own "bare" body, unless it be that in its resurrection it may be no longer bare? That therefore will be additional matter which is placed over the bare body; nor is that at all destroyed on which the superimposed matter is put—nay, it is increased. That, however, is safe which receives augmentation. The truth is, it is sown the barest grain, without a husk to cover it, without a spike even in germ, without the protection of a bearded top, without the glory of a stalk. It rises, however, out of the furrow enriched with a copious crop, built up in a compact fabric, constructed in a beautiful order, fortified by cultivation, and clothed around on every side. These are the circumstances which make it another body from God, to which it is changed not by abolition, but by amplification. And to every seed God has assigned its own body—not, indeed, its own in the sense of its primitive body—in order that what it acquires from God extrinsically may also at last be accounted its own. Cleave firmly then to the example, and keep it well in view, as a mirror of what happens to the flesh: believe that the very same flesh which was once sown in death will bear fruit in resurrection-life—the same in essence, only more full and perfect; not another, although reappearing in another form. For it shall receive in itself the grace and ornament which God shall please to spread over it, according to its merits. Unquestionably it is in this sense that he says, "All flesh is not the same flesh;" meaning not to deny a community of substance, but a parity of prerogative—reducing the body to a difference of honor, not of nature. With this view he adds, in a figurative sense, certain examples of animals and heavenly bodies: "There is one flesh of man" (that is, servants of God, but really human), "another flesh of beasts" (that is, the heathen, of whom the prophet actually says, "Man is like the senseless cattle"), "another flesh of birds" (that is, the martyrs which essay to mount up to heaven), "another of fishes" (that is, those whom the water of baptism has submerged). In like manner does he take examples from the heavenly bodies: "There is one glory of the sun" (that is, of Christ), "and another glory of the moon" (that is, of the Church), "and another glory of the stars" (in other words, of the seed of Abraham). "For one star differeth from another star in glory: so there are bodies terrestrial as well as celestial" (Jews, that is, as well as Christians). Now, if this language is not to be construed figuratively, it was absurd enough for him to make a contrast between the flesh of mules and kites, as well as the heavenly bodies and human bodies; for they admit of no comparison as to their condition, nor in respect of their attainment of a resurrection. Then at last, having conclusively shown by his examples that the difference was one of glory, not of substance, he adds: "So also is the resurrection of the dead." How so? In no other way than as differing in glory only. For again, predicating the resurrection of the same substance and returning once more to (his comparison of) the grain, he says: "It is sown in corruption, it is raised in incorruption; it is sown in dishonor, it is raised in glory; it is sown in weakness, it is raised in power; it is sown a natural body, it is raised a spiritual body." Now, certainly nothing else is raised than that which is sown; and nothing else is sown than that which decays in the ground; and it is nothing else than the flesh which is decayed in the ground. For this was the substance which God's decree demolished, "Earth thou art, and to earth shalt thou return;" because it was taken out of the earth. And it was from this circumstance that the apostle borrowed his phrase of the flesh being "sown," since it returns to the ground, and the ground is the grand depository for seeds which are meant to be deposited in it, and again sought out of it. And therefore he confirms the passage afresh, by putting on it the impress (of his own inspired authority), saying, "For so it is written;" that you may not suppose that the "being sown" means anything else than "thou shalt return to the ground, out of which thou wast taken;" nor that the phrase "for so it is written" refers to any other thing that the flesh.

Chapter LIII. —Not the Soul, But the Natural Body Which Died, is that Which is to Rise Again. The Resurrection of Lazarus Commented on. Christ's Resurrection, as the Second Adam, Guarantees Our Own.

Some, however, contend that the soul is "the natural (or animate) body," with the view of withdrawing the flesh from all connection with the risen body. Now, since it is a clear and fixed point that the body which is to rise again is that which was sown in death, they must be challenged to an examination of the very fact itself. Else let them show that the soul was sown after death; in a word, that it underwent death— that is, was demolished, dismembered, dissolved in the ground, nothing of which was ever decreed against it by God: let them display to our view its corruptibility and dishonor (as well as) its weakness, that it may also accrue to it to rise again in incorruption, and in glory, and in power. Now in the case of Lazarus, (which we may take as) the palmary instance of a resurrection, the flesh lay prostrate in weakness, the flesh was almost putrid in the dishonor of its decay, the flesh stank in corruption, and yet it was as flesh that Lazarus rose again— with his soul, no doubt. But that soul was incorrupt; nobody had wrapped it in its linen swathes; nobody had deposited it in a grave; nobody had yet perceived it "stink;" nobody for four days had seen it "sown." Well, now, this entire condition, this whole end of Lazarus, the flesh indeed of all men is still experiencing, but the soul of no one. That substance, therefore, to which the apostle's whole description manifestly refers, of which he clearly speaks, must be both the natural (or animate) body when it is sown, and the spiritual body when it is raised again. For in order that you may understand it in this sense, he points to this same conclusion, when in like manner, on the authority of the same passage of Scripture, he displays to us "the first man Adam as made a living soul." Now since Adam was the first man, since also the flesh was man prior to the soul it undoubtedly follows that it was the flesh that became the living soul. Moreover, since it was a bodily substance that assumed this condition, it was of course the natural (or animate) body that became the living soul. By what designation would they have it called, except that which it became through the soul, except that which it was not previous to the soul, except that which it can never be after the soul, but through its resurrection? For after it has recovered the soul, it once more becomes the natural (or animate) body, in order that it may become a spiritual body. For it only resumes in the resurrection the condition which it once had. There is therefore by no means the same good reason why the soul should be called the natural (or animate) body, which the flesh has for bearing that designation. The flesh, in fact, was a body before it was an animate body. When the flesh was joined by the soul, it then became the natural (or animate) body. Now, although the soul is a corporeal substance, yet, as it is not an animated body, but rather an animating one, it cannot be called the animate (or natural) body, nor can it become that thing which it produces. It is indeed when the soul accrues to something else that it makes that thing animate; but unless it so accrues, how will it ever produce animation? As therefore the flesh was at first an animate (or natural) body on receiving the soul, so at last will it become a spiritual body when invested with the spirit. Now the apostle, by severally adducing this order in Adam and in Christ, fairly distinguishes between the two states, in the very essentials of their difference. And when he calls Christ "the last Adam," you may from this circumstance discover how strenuously he labors to establish throughout his teaching the resurrection of the flesh, not of the soul. Thus, then, the first man Adam was flesh, not soul, and only afterwards became a living soul; and the last Adam, Christ, was Adam only because He was man, and only man as being flesh, not as being soul. Accordingly, the apostle goes on to say: "Howbeit that was not first which is spiritual, but that which is natural, and afterward that which is spiritual," as in the case of the two Adams. Now, do you not suppose that he is distinguishing between the natural body and the spiritual body in the same flesh, after having already drawn the distinction therein in the two Adams, that is, in the first man and in the last? For from which substance is it that Christ and Adam have a parity with each other? No doubt it is from their flesh, although it may be from their soul also. It is, however, in respect of the flesh that they are both man; for the flesh was man prior to the soul. It was actually from it that they were able to take rank, so as to be deemed—one the first, and the other the last man, or Adam. Besides, things which are different in character are only incapable of being arranged in the same order when their diversity is one of substance; for when it is a diversity either in respect of place, or of time, or of condition, they probably do admit of classification together. Here, however, they are called first and last, from the substance of their (common) flesh, just as afterwards again the first man (is said to be) of the earth, and the second of heaven; but although He is "of heaven" in respect of the spirit, He is yet man according to the flesh. Now since it is the flesh, and not the soul, that makes an order (or classification together) in the two Adams compatible, so that the distinction is drawn between them of "the first man becoming a living soul, and the last a quickening spirit," so in like manner this distinction between them has already suggested the conclusion that the distinction is due to the flesh; so that it is of the flesh that these words speak: "Howbeit that was not first which is spiritual, but that which is natural, and afterward that which is spiritual." And thus, too, the same flesh must be understood in a preceding passage: "That which is sown is the natural body, and that which rises again is the spiritual body; because that is not first which is spiritual, but that which is natural: since the first Adam was made a living soul, the last Adam a quickening spirit." It is all about man, and all about the flesh because about man.

What shall we say then? Has not the flesh even now (in this life) the spirit by faith? so that the question still remains to be asked, how it is that the animate (or natural) body can be said to be sown? Surely the flesh has received even here the spirit—but only its "earnest;" whereas of the soul (it has received) not the earnest, but the full possession. Therefore, it has the name of animate (or natural) body, expressly because of the higher substance of the soul (or anima,) in which it is sown, destined hereafter to become, through the full possession of the spirit which it shall obtain, the spiritual body, in which it is raised again. What wonder, then, if it is more commonly called after the substance with which it is fully furnished, than after that of which it has yet but a sprinkling?

Chapter LIV. —Death Swallowed Up of Life. Meaning of This Phrase in Relation to the Resurrection of the Body.

Then, again, questions very often are suggested by occasional and isolated terms, just as much as they are by connected sentences. Thus, because of the apostle's expression, "that mortality may be swallowed up of life"—in reference to the flesh—they wrest the word swallowed up into the sense of the actual destruction of the flesh; as if we might not speak of ourselves as swallowing bile, or swallowing grief, meaning that we conceal and hide it, and keep it within ourselves. The truth is, when it is written, "This mortal must put on immortality," it is explained in what sense it is that "mortality is swallowed up of life"—even whilst, clothed with immortality, it is hidden and concealed, and contained within it, not as consumed, and destroyed, and lost. But death, you will say in reply to me, at this rate, must be safe, even when it has been swallowed up. Well, then, I ask you to distinguish words which are similar in form according to their proper meanings. Death is one thing, and mortality is another. It is one thing for death to be swallowed up, and another thing for mortality to be swallowed up. Death is incapable of immortality, but not so mortality. Besides, as it is written that "this mortal must put on immortality," how is this possible when it is swallowed up of life? But how is it swallowed up of life, (in the sense of destroyed by it) when it is actually received, and restored, and included in it? For the rest, it is only just and right that death should be swallowed up in utter destruction, since it does itself devour with this same intent. Death, says the apostle, has devoured by exercising its strength, and therefore has been itself devoured in the struggle "swallowed up in victory." "O death, where is thy sting? O death, where is thy victory?" Therefore, life, too, as the great antagonist of death, will in the struggle swallow up for salvation what death, in its struggle, had swallowed up for destruction.

Chapter LV.—The Change of a Thing's Condition is Not the Destruction of Its Substance. The Application of This Principle to Our Subject.

Now although, in proving that the flesh shall rise again we ipso facto prove that no other flesh will partake of that resurrection than that which is in question, yet insulated questions and their occasions do require even discussions of their own, even if they have been already sufficiently met. We will therefore give a fuller explanation of the force and the reason of a change which (is so great, that it) almost suggests the presumption that it is a different flesh which is to rise again; as if, indeed, so great a change amounted to utter cessation, and a complete destruction of the former self. A distinction, however, must be made between a change, however great, and everything which has the character of destruction. For undergoing change is one thing, but being destroyed is another thing. Now this distinction would no longer exist, if the flesh were to suffer such a change as amounts to destruction. Destroyed, however, it must be by the change, unless it shall itself persistently remain throughout the altered condition which shall be exhibited in the resurrection. For precisely as it perishes, if it does not rise again, so also does it equally perish even if it does rise again, on the supposition that it is lost in the change. It will as much fail of a future existence, as if it did not rise again at all. And how absurd is it to rise again for the purpose of not having a being, when it had it in its power not to rise again, and so lose its being—because it had already begun its non-existence! Now, things which are absolutely different, as mutation and destruction are, will not admit of mixture and confusion; in their operations, too, they differ. One destroys, the other changes. Therefore, as that which is destroyed is not changed, so that which is changed is not destroyed. To perish is altogether to cease to be what a thing once was, whereas to be changed is to exist in another condition. Now, if a thing exists in another condition, it can still be the same thing itself; for since it does not perish, it has its existence still. A change, indeed, it has experienced, but not a destruction. A thing may undergo a complete change, and yet remain still the same thing. In like manner, a man also may be quite himself in substance even in the present life, and for all that undergo various changes—in habit, in bodily bulk, in health, in condition, in dignity, and in age—in taste, business, means, houses, laws and customs—and still lose nothing of his human nature, nor so to be made another man as to cease to be the same; indeed, I ought hardly to say another man, but another thing. This form of change even the Holy Scriptures give us instances of. The hand of Moses is changed, and it becomes like a dead one, bloodless, colorless, and stiff with cold; but on the recovery of heat, and on the restoration of its natural color, it is again the same flesh and blood. Afterwards the face of the same Moses is changed, with a brightness which eye could not bear. But he was Moses still, even when he was not visible. So also Stephen had already put on the appearance of an angel, although they were none other than his human knees which bent beneath the stoning. The Lord, again, in the retirement of the mount, had changed His raiment for a robe of light, but He still retained features which Peter could recognize. In that same scene Moses also and Elias gave proof that the same condition of bodily existence may continue even in glory—the one in the likeness of a flesh which he had not yet recovered, the other in the reality of one which he had not yet put off. It was as full of this splendid example that Paul said: "Who shall change our vile body, that it may be fashioned like unto His glorious body." But if you maintain that a transfiguration and a conversion amounts to the annihilation of any substance, then it follows that "Saul, when changed into another man," passed away from his own bodily substance; and that Satan himself, when "transformed into an angel of light," loses his own proper character. Such is not my opinion. So likewise changes, conversions and reformations will necessarily take place to bring about the resurrection, but the substance of the flesh will still be preserved safe.

Chapter LVI—The Procedure of the Last Judgment, and Its Awards, Only Possible on the Identity of the Risen Body with Our Present Flesh.

For how absurd, and in truth how unjust, and in both respects how unworthy of God, for one substance to do the work, and another to reap the reward: that this flesh of ours should be torn by martyrdom, and another wear the crown; or, on the other hand, that this flesh of ours should wallow in uncleanness, and another receive the condemnation! Is it not better to renounce all faith at once in the hope of the resurrection, than to trifle with the wisdom and justice of God? Better that Marcion should rise again than Valentinus. For it cannot be believed that the mind, or the memory, or the conscience of existing man is abolished by putting on that change of raiment which immortality and incorruption supplies; for in that case all the gain and fruit of the resurrection, and the permanent effect of God's judgment both on soul and body, would certainly fall to the ground. If I remember not that it is I who have served Him, how shall I ascribe glory to God? How sing to Him "the new song," if I am ignorant that it is I who owe Him thanks? But why is exception taken only against the change of the flesh, and not of the soul also, which in all things is superior to the flesh? How happens it, that the self-same soul which in our present flesh has gone through all life's course, which has learnt the knowledge of God, and put on Christ, and sown the hope of salvation in this flesh, must reap its harvest in another flesh of which we know nothing? Verily that must be a most highly favored flesh, which shall have the enjoyment of life at so gratuitous a rate! But if the soul is not to be changed also, then there is no resurrection of the soul; nor will it be believed to have itself risen, unless it has risen some different thing.

Chapter LVII—Our Bodies, However Mutilated Before or After Death, Shall Recover Their Perfect Integrity in the Resurrection. Illustration of the Enfranchised Slave.

We now come to the most usual cavil of unbelief. If, they say, it be actually the selfsame substance which is recalled to life with all its form, and lineaments, and quality, then why not with all its other characteristics? Then the blind, and the lame, and the palsied, and whoever else may have passed away with any conspicuous mark, will return again with the same. What now is the fact, although you in the greatness of your conceit thus disdain to accept from God so vast a grace? Does it not happen that, when you now admit the salvation of only the soul, you ascribe it to men at the cost of half their nature? What is the good of believing in the resurrection, unless your faith embraces the whole of it? If the flesh is to be repaired after its dissolution, much more will it be restored after some violent injury. Greater cases prescribe rules for lesser ones. Is not the amputation or the crushing of a limb the death of that limb? Now, if the death of the whole person is rescinded by its resurrection, what must we say of the death of a part of him? If we are changed for glory, how much more for integrity! Any loss sustained by our bodies is an accident to them, but their entirety is their natural property. In this condition we are born. Even if we become injured in the womb, this is loss suffered by what is already a human being. Natural condition is prior to injury. As life is bestowed by God, so is it restored by Him. As we are when we receive it, so are we when we recover it. To nature, not to injury, are we restored; to our state by birth, not to our condition by accident, do we rise again. If God raises not men entire, He raises not the dead. For what dead man is entire, although he dies entire? Who is without hurt, that is without life? What body is uninjured, when it is dead, when it is cold, when it is ghastly, when it is stiff, when it is a corpse? When is a man more infirm, than when he is entirely infirm? When more palsied, than when quite motionless? Thus, for a dead man to be raised again, amounts to nothing short of his being restored to his entire condition—lest he, forsooth, be still dead in that part in which he has not risen again. God is quite able to re-make what He once made. This power and this unstinted grace of His He has already sufficiently guaranteed in Christ; and has displayed Himself to us (in Him) not only as the restorer of the flesh, but as the repairer of its breaches. And so the apostle says: "The dead shall be raised incorruptible" (or unimpaired). But how so, unless they become entire, who have wasted away either in the loss of their health, or in the long decrepitude of the grave? For when he propounds the two clauses, that "this corruptible must put on incorruption, and this mortal must put on immortality," he does not repeat the same statement, but sets forth a distinction. For, by assigning immortality to the repeating of death, and incorruption to the repairing of the wasted body, he has fitted one to the raising and the other to the retrieval of the body. I suppose, moreover, that he promises to the Thessalonians the integrity of the whole substance of man. So that for the great future there need be no fear of blemished or defective bodies. Integrity, whether the result of preservation or restoration, will be able to lose nothing more, after the time that it has given back to it whatever it had lost. Now, when you contend that the flesh will still have to undergo the same sufferings, if the same flesh be said to have to rise again, you rashly set up nature against her Lord, and impiously contrast her law against His grace; as if it were not permitted the Lord God both to change nature, and to preserve her, without subjection to a law. How is it, then, that we read, "With men these things are impossible, but with God all things are possible;" and again, "God hath chosen the foolish things of the world to confound the wise?" Let me ask you, if you were to manumit your slave (seeing that the same flesh and soul will remain to him, which once were exposed to the whip, and the fetter, and the stripes), will it therefore be fit for him to undergo the same old sufferings? I trow not. He is instead thereof honored with the grace of the white robe, and the favor of the gold ring, and the name and tribe as well as table of his patron. Give, then, the same prerogative to God, by virtue of such a change, of reforming our condition, not our nature, by taking away from it all sufferings, and surrounding it with safeguards of protection. Thus our flesh shall remain even after the resurrection—so far indeed susceptible of suffering, as it is the flesh, and the same flesh too; but at the same time impassible, inasmuch as it has been liberated by the Lord for the very end and purpose of being no longer capable of enduring suffering.

Chapter LVIII—From This Perfection of Our Restored Bodies Will Flow the Consciousness of Undisturbed Joy and Peace.

"Everlasting joy," says Isaiah, "shall be upon their heads." Well, there is nothing eternal until after the resurrection. "And sorrow and sighing," continues he, "shall flee away." The angel echoes the same to John: "And God shall wipe away all tears from their eyes;" from the same eyes indeed which had formerly wept, and which might weep again, if the loving-kindness of God did not dry up every fountain of tears. And again: "God shall wipe away all tears from their eyes; and there shall be no more death," and therefore no more corruption, it being chased away by incorruption, even as death is by immortality. If sorrow, and mourning, and sighing, and death itself, assail us from the afflictions both of soul and body, how shall they be removed, except by the cessation of their causes, that is to say, the afflictions of flesh and soul? where will you find adversities in the presence of God? where, incursions of an enemy in the bosom of Christ? where, attacks of the devil in the face of the Holy Spirit?—now that the devil himself and his angels are "cast into the lake of fire." Where now is necessity, and what they call fortune or fate? What plague awaits the redeemed from death, after their eternal pardon? What wrath is there for the reconciled, after grace? What weakness, after their renewed strength? What risk and danger, after their salvation? That the raiment and shoes of the children of Israel remained unworn and fresh for the space of forty years; that in their very persons the exact point of convenience and propriety checked the rank growth of their nails and hair, so that any excess herein might not be attributed to indecency; that the fires of Babylon injured not either the mitres or the trousers of the three brethren, however foreign such dress might be to the Jews; that Jonah was swallowed by the monster of the deep, in whose belly whole ships were devoured, and after three days was vomited out again safe and sound; that Enoch and Elias, who even now, without experiencing a resurrection (because they have not even encountered death), are learning to the full what it is for the flesh to be exempted from all humiliation, and all loss, and all injury, and all disgrace—translated as they have been from this world, and from this very cause already candidates for everlasting life;—to what faith do these notable facts bear witness, if not to that which ought to inspire in us the belief that they are proofs and documents of our own future integrity and perfect resurrection? For, to borrow the apostle's phrase, these were "figures of ourselves;" and they are written that we may believe both that the Lord is more powerful than all natural laws about the body, and that He shows Himself the preserver of the flesh the more emphatically, in that He has preserved for it its very clothes and shoes.

Chapter LIX—Our Flesh in the Resurrection Capable, Without Losing Its Essential Identity, of Bearing the Changed Conditions of Eternal Life, or of Death Eternal.

But, you object, the world to come bears the character of a different dispensation, even an eternal one; and therefore, you maintain, that the non-eternal substance of this life is incapable of possessing a state of such different features. This would be true enough, if man were made for the future dispensation, and not the dispensation for man. The apostle, however, in his epistle says, "Whether it be the world, or life, or death, or things present, or things to come; all are yours:" and he here constitutes us heirs even of the future world. Isaiah gives you no help when he says, "All flesh is grass;" and in another passage, "All flesh shall see the salvation of God." It is the issues of men, not their substances, which he distinguishes. But who does not hold that the judgment of God consists in the twofold sentence, of salvation and of punishment? Therefore, it is that "all flesh is grass," which is destined to the fire; and "all flesh shall see the salvation of God," which is ordained to eternal life. For myself, I am quite sure that it is in no other flesh than my own that I have committed adultery, nor in any other flesh am I striving after continence. If there be any one who bears about in his person two instruments of lasciviousness, he has it in his power, to be sure, to mow down "the grass" of the unclean flesh, and to reserve for himself only that which shall see the salvation of God. But when the same prophet represents to us even nations sometimes estimated as "the small dust of the balance," and as "less than nothing, and vanity," and sometimes as about to hope and "trust in the name" and arm of the Lord, are we at all misled respecting the Gentile nations by the diversity of statement? Are some of them to turn believers, and are others accounted dust, from any difference of nature? Nay, rather Christ has shone as the true light on the nations within the ocean's limits, and from the heaven which is over us all. Why, it is even on this earth that the Valentinians have gone to school for their errors; and there will be no difference of condition, as respects their body and soul, between the nations which believe and those which do not believe. Precisely, then, as He has put a distinction of state, not of nature, amongst the same nations, so also has He discriminated their flesh, which is one and the same substance in those nations, not according to their material structure, but according to the recompense of their merit.

Chapter LX—All the Characteristics of Our Bodies—Sex, Various Limbs, Etc.—Will Be Retained, Whatever Change of Functions These May Have, of Which Point, However, we are No Judges. Analogy of the Repaired Ship.

But behold how persistently they still accumulate their cavils against the flesh, especially against its identity, deriving their arguments even from the functions of our limbs; on the one hand saying that these ought to continue permanently pursuing their labors and enjoyments, as appendages to the same corporeal frame; and on the other hand contending that, inasmuch as the functions of the limbs shall one day come to an end, the bodily frame itself must be destroyed, its permanence without its limbs being deemed to be as inconceivable, as that of the limbs themselves without their functions! What, they ask, will then be the use of the cavity of our mouth, and its rows of teeth, and the passage of the throat, and the branch-way of the stomach, and the gulf of the belly, and the entangled tissue of the bowels, when there shall no longer be room for eating and drinking? What more will there be for these members to take in, masticate, swallow, secrete, digest, eject? Of what avail will be our very hands, and feet, and all our laboring limbs, when even all care about food shall cease? What purpose can be served by loins, conscious of seminal secretions, and all the other organs of generation, in the two sexes, and the laboratories of embryos, and the fountains of the breast, when concubinage, and pregnancy, and infant nurture shall cease? In short, what will be the use of the entire body, when the entire body shall become useless? In reply to all this, we have then already settled the principle that the dispensation of the future state ought not to be compared with that of the present world, and that in the interval between them a change will take place; and we now add the remark, that these functions of our bodily limbs will continue to supply the needs of this life up to the moment when life itself shall pass away from time to eternity, as the natural body gives place to the spiritual, until "this mortal puts on immorality, and this corruptible puts on incorruption:" so that when life shall itself become freed from all wants, our limbs shall then be freed also from their services, and therefore will be no longer wanted. Still, although liberated from their offices, they will be yet preserved for judgment, "that every one may receive the things done in his body." For the judgment-seat of God requires that man be kept entire. Entire, however, he cannot be without his limbs, of the substance of which, not the functions, he consists; unless, forsooth, you will be bold enough to maintain that a ship is perfect without her keel, or her bow, or her stern, and without the solidity of her entire frame. And yet how often have we seen the same ship, after being shattered with the storm and broken by decay, with all her timbers repaired and restored, gallantly riding on the wave in all the beauty of a renewed fabric! Do we then disquiet ourselves with doubt about God's skill, and will, and rights? Besides, if a wealthy ship owner, who does not grudge money merely for his amusement or show, thoroughly repairs his ship, and then chooses that she should make no further voyages, will you contend that the old form and finish is still not necessary to the vessel, although she is no longer meant for actual service, when the mere safety of a ship requires such completeness irrespective of service? The sole question, therefore, which is enough for us to consider here, is whether the Lord, when He ordains salvation for man, intends it for his flesh; whether it is His will that the selfsame flesh shall be renewed. If so, it will be improper for you to rule, from the inutility of its limbs in the future state, that the flesh will be incapable of renovation. For a thing may be renewed, and yet be useless from having nothing to do; but it cannot be said to be useless if it has no existence. If, indeed, it has existence, it will be quite possible for it also not to be useless; it may possibly have something to do; for in the presence of God there will be no idleness.

Chapter LXI—The Details of Our Bodily Sex, and of the Functions of Our Various Members. Apology for the Necessity Which Heresy Imposes of Hunting Up All Its Unblushing Cavils.

Now you have received your mouth, O man, for the purpose of devouring your food and imbibing your drink: why not, however, for the higher purpose of uttering speech, so as to distinguish yourself from all other animals? Why not rather for preaching the gospel of God, that so you may become even His priest and advocate before men? Adam indeed gave their several names to the animals, before he plucked the fruit of the tree; before he ate, he prophesied. Then, again, you received your teeth for the consumption of your meal: why not rather for wreathing your mouth with suitable defense on every opening thereof, small or wide? Why not, too, for moderating the impulses of your tongue, and guarding your articulate speech from failure and violence? Let me tell you, (if you do not know), that there are toothless persons in the world. Look at them, and ask whether even a cage of teeth be not an honor to the mouth. There are apertures in the lower regions of man and woman, by means of which they gratify no doubt their animal passions; but why are they not rather regarded as outlets for the cleanly discharge of natural fluids? Women, moreover, have within them receptacles where human seed may collect; but are they not designed for the secretion of those sanguineous issues, which their tardier and weaker sex is inadequate to disperse? For even details like these require to be mentioned, seeing that heretics single out what parts of our bodies may suit them, handle them without delicacy, and, as their whim suggests, pour torrents of scorn and contempt upon the natural functions of our members, for the purpose of upsetting the resurrection, and making us blush over their cavils; not reflecting that before the functions cease, the very causes of them will have passed away. There will be no more meat, because no more hunger; no more drink, because no more thirst; no more concubinage, because no more child-bearing; no more eating and drinking, because no more labor and toil. Death, too, will cease; so there will be no more need of the nutriment of food for the defense of life, nor will mothers' limbs any longer have to be laden for the replenishment of our race. But even in the present life there may be cessations of their office for our stomachs and our generative organs. For forty days Moses and Elias fasted, and lived upon God alone. For even so early was the principle consecrated: "Man shall not live by bread alone, but by every word that proceedeth out of the mouth of God." See here faint outlines of our future strength! We even, as we may be able, excuse our mouths from food, and withdraw our sexes from union. How many voluntary eunuchs are there! How many virgins espoused to Christ! How many, both of men and women, whom nature has made sterile, with a structure which cannot procreate! Now, if even here on earth both the functions and the pleasures of our members may be suspended, with an intermission which, like the dispensation itself, can only be a temporary one, and yet man's safety is nevertheless unimpaired, how much more, when his salvation is secure, and especially in an eternal dispensation, shall we not cease to desire those things, for which, even here below, we are not unaccustomed to check our longings!

Chapter LXII—Our Destined Likeness to the Angels in the Glorious Life of the Resurrection.

To this discussion, however, our Lord's declaration puts an effectual end: "They shall be," says He, "equal unto the angels." As by not marrying, because of not dying, so, of course, by not having to yield to any like necessity of our bodily state; even as the angels, too, sometimes. were "equal unto" men, by eating and drinking, and submitting their feet to the washing of the bath—having clothed themselves in human guise, without the loss of their own intrinsic nature. If therefore angels, when they became as men, submitted in their own unaltered substance of spirit to be treated as if they were flesh, why shall not men in like manner, when they become "equal unto the angels," undergo in their unchanged substance of flesh the treatment of spiritual beings, no more exposed to the usual solicitations of the flesh in their angelic garb, than were the angels once to those of the spirit when encompassed in human form? We shall not therefore cease to continue in the flesh, because we cease to be importuned by the usual wants of the flesh; just as the angels ceased not therefore to remain in their spiritual substance, because of the suspension of their spiritual incidents. Lastly, Christ said not, "They shall be angels," in order not to repeal their existence as men; but He said, "They shall be equal unto the angels," that He might preserve their humanity unimpaired. When He ascribed an angelic likeness to the flesh, He took not from it its proper substance.

Chapter LXIII. —Conclusion. The Resurrection of the Flesh in Its Absolute Identity and Perfection. Belief of This Had Become Weak. Hopes for Its Refreshing Restoration Under the Influences of the Paraclete.

And so the flesh shall rise again, wholly in every man, in its own identity, in its absolute integrity. Wherever it may be, it is in safe keeping in God's presence, through that most faithful "Mediator between God and man, (the man) Jesus Christ," who shall reconcile both God to man, and man to God; the spirit to the flesh, and the flesh to the spirit. Both natures has He already united in His own self; He has fitted them together as bride and bridegroom in the reciprocal bond of wedded life. Now, if any should insist on making the soul the bride, then the flesh will follow the soul as her dowry. The soul shall never be an outcast, to be had home by the bridegroom bare and naked. She has her dower, her outfit, her fortune in the flesh, which shall accompany her with the love and fidelity of a foster sister. But suppose the flesh to be the bride, then in Christ Jesus she has in the contract of His blood received His Spirit as her spouse. Now, what you take to be her extinction, you may be sure is only her temporary retirement. It is not the soul only which withdraws from view. The flesh, too, has her departures for a while—in waters, in fires, in birds, in beasts; she may seem to be dissolved into these, but she is only poured into them, as into vessels. And should the vessels themselves afterwards fail to hold her, escaping from even these, and returning to her mother earth, she is absorbed once more, as it were, by its secret embraces, ultimately to stand forth to view, like Adam when summoned to hear from his Lord and Creator the words, "Behold, the man is become as one of us!"— thoroughly "knowing" by that time "the evil" which she had escaped, "and the good" which she has acquired. Why, then, O soul, should you envy the flesh? There is none, after the Lord, whom you should love so dearly; none more like a brother to you, which is even born along with yourself in God. You ought rather to have been by your prayers obtaining resurrection for her: her sins, whatever they were, were owing to you. However, it is no wonder if you hate her; for you have repudiated her Creator. You have accustomed yourself either to deny or change her existence even in Christ—corrupting the very Word of God Himself, who became flesh, either by mutilating or misinterpreting the Scripture, and introducing, above all, apocryphal mysteries and blasphemous fables. But yet Almighty God, in His most gracious providence, by "pouring out of His Spirit in these last days, upon all flesh, upon His servants and on His handmaidens," has checked these impostures of unbelief and perverseness, reanimated men's faltering faith in the resurrection of the flesh, and cleared from all obscurity and equivocation the ancient Scriptures (of both God's Testaments) by the clear light of their (sacred) words and meanings. Now, since it was "needful that there should be heresies, in order that they which are approved might be made manifest;" since, however, these heresies would be unable to put on a bold front without some countenance from the Scriptures, it therefore is plain enough that the ancient Holy Writ has furnished them with sundry materials for their evil doctrine, which very materials indeed (so distorted) are refutable from the same Scriptures. It was fit and proper, therefore, that the Holy Ghost should no longer withhold the effusions of His gracious light upon these inspired writings, in order that they might be able to disseminate the seeds of truth with no admixture of heretical subtleties, and pluck out from it their tares. He has accordingly now dispersed all the perplexities of the past, and their self-chosen allegories and parables, by the open and perspicuous explanation of the entire mystery, through the new prophecy, which descends in copious streams from the Paraclete. If you will only draw water from

His fountains, you will never thirst for other doctrine: no feverish craving after subtle questions will again consume you; but by drinking in evermore the resurrection of the flesh, you will be satisfied with the refreshing draughts.

Elucidations.

I.

(Cadaver, cap. xviii. p. 588.)

The Schoolmen and middle-age jurists improved on Tertullian's etymology. He says,—"a cadendo—cadaver." But they form the word thus: Caro data vermibus = Ca-da-ver.

On this subject see a most interesting discourse of the (paradoxical and sophistical, nay the whimsical) Count Joseph de Maistre, in his Soirées de St. Pétersbourg. He remarks on the happy formation of many Latin words, in this manner: e.g., Cæcus ut ire = Cæcutire, "to grope like a blind man." The French, he says, are not without such examples, and he instances the word ancêtre = ancestor, as composed out of ancien and être, i.e., one of a former existence. Courage, he says, is formed from cæurand rage, this use of rage being the Greek θυμος. He supposes that the English use the word rage in this sense, but I recall only the instance:

"Chill penury repressed their noble rage,"

from Gray's Elegy. The Diversions of Purley, of Horne-Tooke, supply amusing examples of the like in the formation of English words.

II.

(His flesh, the Bread, cap. xxxvii. p. 572.)

Note our author's exposition. He censures those who understood our Lord's words after the letter, as if they were to eat the carnal body. He expounds the spiritual thing which gives life as to be understood by the text: "the words that I speak unto you, they are spirit and they are life." His word is the life-giving principle and therefore he called his flesh by the same name: and we are to "devour Him with the ear and to ruminate on Him with the understanding, and to digest Him by faith." The flesh profits nothing, the spirit imparts life. Now, was Tertullian ever censured for this exposition? On the contrary, this was the faith of the Catholic Church, from the beginning. Our Saxon forefathers taught the same, as appears from the Homily of Ælfric, a.d.980, and from the exposition of Ratramn, a.d.840. The heresy of Transubstantiation was not dogmatic even among Latins, until the Thirteenth century, and it prevailed in England less than three hundred years, when the Catholic doctrine was restored, through the influence of Ratramn's treatise first upon the mind of Ridley and then by Ridley's arguments with Cranmer. Thus were their understandings opened to the Scriptures and to the acknowledging of the Truth, for which they suffered martyrdom. To the reformation we owe the rescue of Ante-Nicene doctrine from the perversions of the Schoolmen and the gradual corruptions of doctrine after the Ninth Century.

III.

(Paradise, cap. xliii. p. 576.)

This sentence reads, in the translation I am editing, as follows: "No one, on becoming absent from the body, is at once a dweller in the presence of the Lord, except by the prerogative of martyrdom, whereby (the saint) gets at once a lodging in Paradise, not in Hades." But the original does not say precisely this, nor does the author use the Greek word Hades. His words are: "Nemo enim peregrinatus a corpore statim immoratur penes Dominum nisi ex martyrii prœrogativa Paradiso silicet non Inferis diversurus." The passage therefore, is not necessarily as inconsistent with the author's topography of the invisible world, as might seem. "Not in the regions beneath Paradise but in Paradise itself," seems to be the idea; Paradise being included in the world of Hades, indeed, but in a lofty region, far enough removed from the Inferi, and refreshed by light from the third Heaven and the throne itself, (as this planet is by the light of the Sun,) immensely distant though it be from the final abode of the Redeemed.